THE
WIN

Knowing and
Pursuing
Our Destination

THE
WIN

Knowing and Pursuing Our Destination

By
Fred Campbell

TOWNSEND**PRESS**

SUNDAY SCHOOL PUBLISHING BOARD

330 CHARLOTTE AVENUE | NASHVILLE, TN 37201-1188

Official Publisher for the National Baptist Convention, USA, Inc.

ISBN: 978-1-939225-35-1

TABLE OF CONTENTS

TABLE OF CONTENTS

INTRODUCTION

Many churches have learned to be efficient in doing church ineffectively. While churches are actively engaged in writing and displaying purpose, vision, and strategy statements, they often stall in their pursuit of the same. Growth strategists are constantly publishing books that focus on methodologies of church growth, while at the same time church attendance is declining, thus causing panic in Christendom. In an effort to stop such a decline in attendance, strategists have shifted the focus from Christ's methods for growing His church to human methods. However, within that atmosphere of panic it is comforting to know that the church belongs to Christ; He purchased it with His own blood. Therefore, we dare not panic. Although some suggest that this is a post-church era where there is a cry for a churchless Christianity, the fact remains that the church does belong to Christ.

Declining churches are facing impending death, and they are desperately searching for new methods to extricate themselves from this valley of death. One such method encouraged by self-proclaimed church growth experts is to keep the same message, but couch it within different methods. These experts say that if the church is to survive, she must do ministry differently. Some espouse that a new kind of church is imperative in the twenty-first century. This new kind of church is one that is designed for the unchurched—a church that is user-friendly. Granted, we are in a different and difficult era which demands change, but I must wonder if we are overreacting. I also wonder if we have abandoned the first century methodology of growing Christ's church simply to appease the unchurched. Thom S. Rainer and Eric Geiger, in their book titled, *Simple Church*, call for the church to return to God's plan for making disciples.

At the risk of sounding cynical, I must say that many of the new church growth methods have limited biblical precedent. Some of these methods make gatherings and/or places of worship the center of evangelism.

Members are encouraged to invite rather than evangelize, thus making the method for reaching the lost world for Christ more of a "come ye," instead of a "go ye," the latter being the method commanded by Christ in the Great Commandment and Commission—a method that cannot and should not be considered obsolete or outdated. However, by merely inviting, churches have become monastic rather than missional and appear to have given up on "as you go make disciples."[1]

The seeker-sensitive method is better than doing nothing—although it is not a biblical model—and it does not warrant disdain from those who may disagree with it because, agree or disagree, it is a method by which people are coming to Christ. But Jesus' method of reaching the world is His mandate for His church to take the Gospel into the world—a world in which we work, live, play, and learn.

While church leaders and growth strategist are troubled and deeply concerned by the supposed impending death of the church as a result of declining church attendance, as mentioned above, the methodologies they put in place to grow the church seem to reflect that they are more desirous of quantity rather than quality. It appears that they are concerned more about counting members than weighing them. This brings up the question: Is the Christian church in trouble simply because the numbers are dropping? We must examine who is leaving the church, and why. Have we considered that perhaps "they went out from us, because they were not of us; for if they had been of us, they would no doubt have continued with us: but they went out, that they might be made manifest that they were not of us"?[2]

I am not suggesting that members who leave the fellowship of the church are leaving because they are not authentic believers—that they are merely goats in sheep's clothing. I am aware that there are various reasons

---

1 The Bible: Matthew 28:19a

2 The Bible: 1 John 2:19

why members leave the fellowship. Weak, immature believers may leave the fellowship because they have been neglected and hurt deeply. Persecution causes membership decline. Members who are actually goats will abandon the fellowship when under pressure. Yet another reason why members leave the fellowship is that they feel their needs are not being met by the church.

I do not want to sound pessimistic or by any means discourage evangelistic fervor, but the decline of membership might be a reminder of the remnant that Jesus spoke of in His discourse on judging. Here are His words: "Enter through the narrow gate. For wide is the gate and broad is the road that leads to destruction, and many enter through it. But small is the gate and narrow the road that leads to life and only a few find it."[3]

Decline and death of local congregations have occurred throughout church history. The New Testament churches that salted and peppered the lands of Asia Minor are nearly, if not altogether, nonexistent. The fact that the church is waning in polytheistic and postmodern America should not be a surprise to us. This is not to suggest, however, that we should become pessimistic and complacent, or think there is nothing wrong with the church and not be concerned about the decline in church membership and attendance. There is unhealthiness in some modern churches that lends to the decline. Some churches are in danger of being spit out of Jesus' mouth.[4] They are dysfunctional and ineffective in living out Christ's mandate for His church, and I boldly suggest that these congregations need to consider merging or joining functional congregations to form a stronger presence in their communities.

There are other local congregations that are unhealthy and simply need to disband because their inception is the result of a conflict or split that occurred within another congregation. Congregations formed in this ungodly way are not as healthy as congregations that are intentionally,

---

3 The Bible: Matthew 7:13-14, NIV

4 The Bible: Revelation 3:16

strategically, purposefully, and prayerfully planted. That a local church disbands and dies is a contradiction to Jesus' promise that "the gates of hell shall not prevail against [the church]."[5] The local church congregation is not the same as "the church" of which Jesus speaks in this verse. The church of which Christ speaks is His church, the body of believers, the bride of Christ, and Christ's church will never dissolve, decline, or die. Christ's church has and will survive, and her survival does not depend on us but on "Him who is able to keep the church from falling and presenting her blameless before His glory with great joy, to the only God, our Savior, through Jesus Christ our Lord, be glory, majesty, dominion, and authority, before all time and now and forever, Amen."[6]

While we may be stewards of His church, Christ is Lord of His church. Christ loves His church, His bride. He gave His life that she might exist, and He rose from the grave that she might effectively exist until He presents her to Himself in splendor, without spot or wrinkle or any such thing, that she might be holy and without blemish (see Ephesians 5:25-27). My prayer is that congregations struggling to survive will consolidate, collaborate, or cooperate for the sake of the body and bride of Christ. However consolidation, collaboration, and cooperation do not automatically lead to effectiveness.

A clear understanding of the church's destination must drive the church. Organizing around the purpose, vision, and strategy statements, the destination should be described in the purpose statement. The purpose statement should clearly state the purpose of the church's existence, but this is often not the case. Most purpose and vision statements fall short of describing the destination—a destination towards the win. They stall at the means rather than the end.

---

5 The Bible: Matthew 16:18b, ESV

6 The Bible: Jude 24, 25

Leadership presupposes or takes for granted that a destination is automatically assumed. While attending a leadership conference, I asked some pastors where they were going as leaders. What was their destination? A lot of their answers were superficial. Many of them had no clue where they were headed. A leader with no sense of direction is lost. They often sense the responsibility of keeping their followers together without a sense of divine direction.

For most leaders and Christians alike, the destination is simply getting to heaven. They exclaim if they can just make it into heaven they will be satisfied, or they say if they could just behold the face of Jesus, they will be satisfied. To be in heaven with Jesus is their destination. There is nothing wrong with looking forward to that glorious day when we will be with Jesus and behold His wonderful face. However, we ought not to forget that our journey is one that begins at regeneration, continues through sanctification, and ultimately ends in glorification. Along this journey, leaders must be destined to fulfill their responsibility of leading Christians towards being like Jesus. In order for leaders to fulfill this task, they must possess character qualifications (see 1 Timothy 3:1-13; Titus 1:5-9). It is the destination (Christians' becoming like Christ) that determines the vital need for these character qualifications in leaders. Credentials and charisma are helpful, but character is essential.

Secularly, sports teams have one common goal: to win. And it is not just to win as many games as possible throughout the season, but to ultimately win the big championship. In basketball, it is winning the NBA Finals; in football, it is winning the Super Bowl; in baseball, it is winning the World Series; in soccer, it is winning the World Cup; and in hockey, it is winning the Stanley Cup. The team, its owners, managers, coaches, trainers, and cheerleaders all work as a team to accomplish their common goal.

Spiritually, on the other hand, from my vantage point most churches are dysfunctional because, unlike sports teams, their common goal is either nonexistent or unclear. Therefore, instead of being unified as the body of Christ the members and ministries of these churches conduct themselves independently of the head which results in a body that is disorderly and epileptic; the church becomes efficient in doing church ineffectively.

In other words, these churches do not have the win as their common goal. They are unaware of what the win is. They have determined their own win and destination instead of seeking to accomplish Christ's "championship" win. Teams that win championships have players and staff who are on the same page. Church members and leaders must be on the same page in order to achieve the win.

Andy Stanley, Reggie Joiner, and Land Jones coauthored a book titled *7 Practices of Effective Ministry*, which prompted the title and focus of this literary discipline. I was captivated by the simplistic approach to ministry detailed in the book. The authors speak of a planned encounter that a local pastor had with the owner of the Atlanta Braves baseball team at a game. This baseball owner had a winning strategy for being effective in business. This strategy, if applied to the church, would result in an effective ministry. I almost lost interest in finishing the book, but the question posed to the young pastor by the owner captured my attention: "How do you clarify the win, and what is the most important thing?" Once "the most important thing" is defined, then you can best "clarify the win." This was the owner's strategy for an effective business.

The Mount Zion Baptist Church in Redwood City, California adopted their win strategy from the North Point Community Church in Atlanta, Georgia. The pastor, leaders, and congregation prayed for clarity as they crafted the following win statement, a statement that drives and directs the members and the ministries of the congregation:

> "We win when each member grows in relationship with Jesus, being, doing, thinking like Him, influencing growth and maturity in the body of Christ."

This book will define this win statement as a discipleship strategy for fulfilling the Great Commandment and Commission. The commandments to "love" and "go" are not suggestions posed to the church of Jesus Christ. The imperative to love empowers the church to go into the world with the Gospel of grace. On our way to the world, we must go by the church. We are not to stay at the church, but we are to prepare there for the sake of the world. We are not of the world, but we are called to live and minister in the world to the glory of God and the salvation of the lost.

Lend me your mind and heart as we pursue the win that has been won in Jesus our Lord and Savior. Prayerfully read *The Win: Knowing and Pursuing Our Destination,* beginning with regeneration and culminating in our glorification through Jesus Christ predicated on His finished work.

CHAPTER

1

Body Life: The Mysterious Relationship

"We win when each member grows in relationship with Jesus, being, doing, thinking like Him, influencing growth and maturity in the body of Christ."

We Christians often struggle to form an accurate idea of church membership. We do so because we think in terms of organization instead of organism. Attitudes and behavior within congregations would be transformed to the glory of God and the edification of the saints if we thought in terms of body life. One of the fundamental doctrines of the apostle Paul was oneness in the body of Christ:

"For as we, being many members in one body, but all the members do not have the same function, so we, being many, are one body in Christ, and individually members of one another" (Romans 12:4-5, NKJV).

Jesus and the apostles described the Christian experience as entering "one another-ness" (see John 13:34; Hebrews 10:24; 1 Peter 1:22; 4:9; 5:14; 1 John 3:11; 3:23; 4:7, 11-12).

God's purpose and action in salvation is to call sinners unto Himself through the atoning sacrifice of His Son, justifying, sanctifying, and incorporating them into "one another-ness"—the body of Christ. This is the mystery that was once hidden from view but is now revealed in the life of the church—the body of Christ comprised of Jews and Gentiles.

"For He Himself is our peace, who has made both one, and has broken down the middle wall of separation, having abolished in His flesh the enmity, that is, the law of commandments contained in ordinances, so as to create in Himself one new man from the two, thus making peace, and that He might reconcile them both to God in one body through the cross, thereby putting to death the enmity. And He came and preached peace to you who were afar off and to those who were near. For through Him we both have access by one Spirit to the Father" (Ephesians 2:14-18, NKJV).

The only true God who created the universe created one body in the world to replace His only begotten Son. The mystery of the church is in the nature of its membership—Jews and Gentiles. And the means of its membership is to be baptized by one Spirit into relationship with one another. *"For by one Spirit we were all baptized into one body—whether Jews or Greeks, whether slaves or free—and have all been made to drink into one Spirit"* (1 Corinthians 12:13, NKJV). This mysterious union of plural oneness is indispensable and is reflective of the Trinity and illustrated in Christian marriage. The apostle Paul connects these mysteries by stating the following:

"For we are members of His body, of His flesh and of His bones. 'For this reason a man shall leave his father and mother and be joined to his wife, and the two shall become one flesh.' This is a great mystery, but I speak concerning Christ and the church. Nevertheless let each one of you in particular so love his own wife as himself, and let the wife see that she respects her husband" (Ephesians 5:30-33, NKJV).

"And without controversy great is the mystery of godliness: God was manifest in the Spirit, seen of angels, preached unto the Gentiles, believed on in the world, received up to glory" (1 Timothy 3:16, KJV).

The mysteries of the Godhead, the church, and marriage are that of plural oneness.

The Birth by the Holy Spirit

Fundamentally, the mystery of the church is each member's personal relationship with Christ the head of the church, and an interpersonal relationship with one another (see Ephesians 4:11-16). Because believers come from the same spiritual womb, we are spiritual siblings. The origin of our new birth is the Holy Spirit (see John 3:5-6), and God is our Father. The nature of our new birth is the life of the Son (see 1 John 5:11-12). The Bible does not teach the universal fatherhood of God.

People are not automatically qualified to be called sons of God simply because He created us all. Believers are called sons of God because we are of Abraham's seed (see John 8:31-59). And as Nicodemus learned in John 3:1-8, natural birth does not qualify one for sonship with the Father, neither does simply adhering to the teachings of Jesus Christ. Only spiritual birth qualifies one for sonship (see John 1:9-13). When we have been birthed into the family of God, we are then true brothers and sisters in Christ. It is a matter of regeneration, not reformation.

Family is a good metaphor for the church and how we became members is miraculous, but we are more than members of God's family. We are also members of Christ's body, another metaphor of a spiritual reality. Yes we are family, but it is more intimate than family ties. It is many members forming one glorious body, the church. We came forth from the same womb and are strategically placed into this one body. As spiritual siblings, we form one new family but moreover, one new man (see Ephesians 2:14-18).

The Baptism of the Holy Spirit

We as the church, the body of Christ, on the whole do not understand the dynamics of the interrelated nature of the church. We misuse, misrepresent, and mismanage the affairs and fellowship of the church because we are unaware of the reality of body life. In 1 Corinthians 3:16-17, the apostle Paul blatantly warns the Corinthian fellowship as he addresses divisions in the church:

"Do you not know that you are God's temple and that God's Spirit dwells in you? If anyone destroys God's temple, God will destroy him. For God's temple is holy, and you are that temple" (ESV).

I do not believe Paul is referring to individual believers in this passage, as he did in 1 Corinthians 6:19-20. I believe that he is referring to the unified, corporate church. Corporate unity is the answer to Jesus' intercessory prayer for believers, found in John 17. Therefore, unity need not be sought after but maintained (see Ephesians 4:3) because it is a result of the Spirit's baptism, which is automatic at the initial salvation experience when believers are also baptized into the body of Christ (not to be confused with water baptism).

While water baptism is an act of our obedience, Jesus baptizes with the Holy Spirit, which is instantaneous at salvation. John the Baptist said, *"I indeed baptize you with water unto repentance, but He who is coming after me is mightier than I, whose sandals I am not worthy to carry. He will baptize you with the Holy Spirit and fire"* (Matthew 3:11, ESV).

The apostle Paul describes this baptism that Jesus performs through the Holy Spirit as a means of placing believers into the body of Christ. It is not a second blessing of the Spirit. There are no commands in Scripture for believers to seek the baptism of the Spirit. We are commanded to be controlled by the Spirit (see Ephesians 5:18), but not to be baptized by the Spirit.

The baptism of the Spirit is a supernatural, dynamic, and essential occurrence that all believers experience. It is not some sensational extra experience in salvation, such as speaking in tongues. In fact, speaking in tongues (language) is a gift, and this gift need not be manifested to authenticate the reality of the baptism of the Spirit. Baptism of the Spirit is not exclusive to a particular group of people. All believers experience this spiritual phenomenon at the point of salvation.

"For by one Spirit are we all baptized into one body, whether we be Jews or Gentiles, whether we be bond or free; and have been all made to drink into one Spirit" (1 Corinthians 12:13, KJV).

Baptism of the Spirit is an individual experience that results in a corporate experience—plural oneness. The baptism experience places believers into an indispensable union with one another. We are baptized into the "one another-ness." We are connected (joined together) with each other and with Christ the head of the church.

Plural oneness of the church transcends the notion of a team, an organization, or a family. Plural oneness is not an ideological oneness or oneness in thought. It is not a mere purposeful oneness that moves us in the same direction as a group of individuals. No! We speak of an organic relationship, body life, members of one another, diversity in unity. It is not merely an organization, but rather an organism; that is plural oneness.

With plural oneness, there can be no churchless Christianity. The baptism of the Holy Spirit is not optional or conditional. It is the reality of the salvation experience. A Christian is called to live out the new life in relationship with other Christians. We must live with the awareness that God is *our* Father. For Jesus, God is *His* Father in a unique sense, but to the Christian God is *our* Father in a corporate sense. He can be *my* Father in a personal sense but never in the unique sense as He is to Jesus (see John 3:16).

While this Father and sonship relationship is individual (see John 1:12-13), it is always plural (see 1 John 3:1-3). A Christian may disconnect from a local congregation, but it is impossible to disconnect from the body of Christ. Now this statement must not be understood as supporting Christians living in isolation from other Christians in some churchless society. Although the body of Christ is a tremendous mystery, it is not some mythological, metaphorical reality. The church is comprised of organized and orderly local congregations of many members, which is the way the church is to function (see 1 Corinthians 12:12-31; 14:26-40). As the human body is orderly, so is the body of Christ (the church), and local congregations are microcosms of the body of Christ; however, some Christians scoff at the orderly, organized local congregation in favor of one that is disorganized or loosely organized.

The church is the bride of Christ and He only has one bride. He does not practice polygamy; He is not a bigamist. Therefore, we can only relate to Christ as His bride in connection with other believers. I have a holy-hunch that in heaven our relationship with Christ will be as His bride—not just as individuals, but as a corporate body. The church as body and bride is an obvious teaching of Paul in Ephesians 5. These metaphoric descriptions of the church are contextualized in plural oneness. The corporate nature of the church, I believe, will continue in eternity. In some way, the Old Testament saints and the New Testament saints will gather in this plural oneness in the Holy City (see Revelation 21).

The birth of the church is the formation of a new man (see Ephesians 2:11-22). This speaks of the church as an organism. Corporately, the church is the witness unto Christ in the world (see Acts 1:8). The witness is ontological, in that the church is the reappearance of Christ. Christ is back on the planet through His church. I think that this is what Paul was saying when he wrote these words:

"And hath put all things under his [Christ's] feet, and gave him [Christ] to be head over all things to the church, which is His body, the fullness of Him that filleth all in all" (Ephesians 1:22-23, KJV).

As one body, the church is the fullness of Christ, who is alive in every member of the body. His life flows through every part of the body. We are strategically placed into the body. *"From whom the whole body fitly joined together and compacted by that which every joint supplieth, according to the effectual working in the measure of every part, maketh increase of the body unto the edifying of itself in love"* (Ephesians 4:16, KJV).

The purpose of the strategic placements is to manifest Christ on earth. John MacArthur says, "The church is the fullness or complement of Christ. As a head must have a body to manifest the glory of that head, so the Lord must have the church to manifest His glory."[7]

The Indispensable Relationship

"We win when each member grows in relationship with Jesus, being, doing, thinking like Him, influencing growth and maturity in the body of Christ."

The "we" in the statement above refers to our indispensable union in the body of Christ. Previously, I alluded to this relational mystery that renders the church one body with many members, but now I shall elaborate further. Conflicts and fighting within the fellowship arise when there is little or no sense of body life. The church at Corinth is a case in point. The saints in Corinth were dysfunctional as part of the body of Christ. Division, strife, misunderstanding and misuse of gifts, and unchallenged and unconfessed sins all hindered body life in the church (see 1 Corinthians 3:16-17). Paul teaches that the church is holy and must not be trifled with; however, the church was and still is being mishandled and mistreated. I think our failure to teach and impress upon the church the reality of interrelationships in the church causes us to behave unappreciatively.

Membership in the church must not be viewed as insignificant. I believe that sometimes we innocently suggest that discipleship is better

---

7 John MacArthur, The MacArthur New Testament Commentary, Ephesians (Chicago: Moody Press, 1986, p.49)

than membership in the church, not realizing the dynamics of our relationships in the organism. We often make a distinction between organism and organization when, in fact, there is order in organism. There can be no life in an organization, but there cannot be life in an organism without some form of organization. Now it is true that you can join a local congregation (the organization) without being born into the body of Christ (the organism). In other words, you can be a mere member of the local congregation without being a real member of the body of Christ.

The term *member* must not be minimized by suggesting that membership is less than discipleship. We must clarify the point that inorganic membership is one thing, but organic membership in the body of Christ is the dynamic work of Christ through the agency of the Holy Spirit. Christians are referred to as members (see Romans 12:4-5). We are not mere members, but specifically members one of another. Having your name listed on a congregation's membership roll is quite different from having your name written in the Lamb's book of life.

We must be careful as well to not minimize biblical church membership. Active, biblical church membership is more than just being involved with and participating in the affairs and ministries of a local congregation. Active, biblical church membership must be the experience of birth and baptism of the Holy Spirit with members operating in their gifts while bearing the fruit of the Spirit for the edification of the body of Christ (see 1 Corinthians 12–13). The operation of gifts in the body have to do with relationships. The Holy Spirit gives gifts for the sake of the body, not for the sake of the individual member; and when members are not concerned with the life of the body, gifts are misused, as was the case with the Corinthian church and with churches today. Body life is absent in a church where Christians are: 1) functioning independently of other believers, 2) self-centered, and, 3) absorbed in self-interest rather than self-denial.

Body life is present in a church where there are grace-driven Christians. Grace-driven Christians are the opposite of Christians functioning independently of other believers. Grace-driven Christians focus on others in the body of Christ, which is just the opposite of being self-centered. Every member in the body of Christ must live for the sake of the whole. The body is handicapped when members lose sight of the fact that we are fellow heirs, fellow members, fellow partakers, and fellow citizens. Also, grace-driven Christians are willing to deny self in lieu of seeking to have their own self-interests satisfied. Self-denial requires sacrifice and suffering for righteousness' sake. Self-denial is not popular in congregations these days. Self-denial brings on feelings of discomfort which is quite the opposite of why people follow God in this modern age. People seek God to be served by Him rather than to be of service to Him.

"For I say through the grace given me, to everyone who is among you, not to think of himself more highly than he ought to think, but to think soberly, as God has dealt to each one a measure of faith. For as we have many members in one body, but all the members do not have the same function, so we, being many are one body in Christ, and individually members of one another" (Romans 12:3-5, NKJV).

Independence, self-centeredness, and self-absorption in the body of Christ equate to an absence of love, and when there is no love, there is no fellowship, which renders the gifts of the body ineffective (see 1 Corinthians 13:1-3). How can we best get the world to believe in Jesus? While preaching, teaching, and evangelism is essential to sinners' believing in Jesus, loving one another is quintessential. *"A new commandment I give to you, that you love one another. By this all will know that you are my disciples, if you have love for one another"* (John 13:34-35, NKJV).

The body of Christ is identified with Him through loving one another. Spiritual gifts are given to enhance relationships in the body in order that Christ may be visible to the world. Where is God? That is a question that many people are asking. The answer is: God is at home in His church, and we are members of His household. The apostle Paul wrote, *"In whom you also are being built together for a dwelling place of God in the Spirit"* (Ephesians 2:22, NKJV).

Paul's metaphoric description of the church as a physical body is expounded upon in 1 Corinthians 12:12-26. This "one another-ness" in this indispensable union is made clear in this passage. Through the incarnation, God produced one Christ. Now through the reincarnation, God produced one body of Christ. The crucifixion did not rid the world of Christ; it was the means of producing His church, His body. Therefore, through His church Christ is back in business in the world. There is diversity in unity by divine design. As every member of the physical body is unique, calling not for uniformity but functionality, so is the body of Christ. The level of immaturity among the Corinthian church members was evidenced by some members' feeling superior and others feeling inferior. Instead of caring for each other, members were competing, comparing, and complaining. The backstage or behind-the-scenes members thought they were not important, while the onstage or in-the-limelight members thought more highly of themselves than they should have. Paul challenged them not to rebel against the mind and wisdom of God. They were where they were in the body because it pleased God. It is a matter of grace to be a member of the body of Christ. You and I ought to be thankful that we are in His body, regardless of where that may be. What a privilege it is to belong to the collective presence of Christ on earth. The plural oneness of the church must be rescued from this self-serving, self-centered teaching that is permeating the church these days.

The work of parachurch ministries would fare far better if we thought of ourselves in terms of one body of Christ, especially our denominational bodies. I understand the need for autonomy of local congregations in relation to larger denominational bodies, but that very independence somehow keeps us from operating as one body. How can we have both diversity and unity in the body of Christ through denominationalism? If we are to be effective in denominational work, we must have the mindset of organism, not merely organization. Also, if local congregations are to be more effective, they must think in terms of "we" and not "me" or "my." Remember, *"We win when each member grows in relationship with Jesus, being, doing, thinking like Him, influencing growth and maturity in the body of Christ."*

Think It Through

1. How will the idea of plural oneness affect your attitude and behavior in your interpersonal relationships in your local congregation?

2. Why is oneness so important to God?

3. How does it affect you to know that you are a vital part of Christ's exclusive presence in the world?

4. What is the difference between the supernatural and a sensational baptism of the Spirit?

5. Why is it unnecessary to seek unity, but to maintain it in the body of Christ?

6. Explain the idea of the church as the reincarnation of Jesus.

7. How will knowing that your interpersonal relationships in your local congregation are an indispensable union help to maintain unity in your church?

8. How does self-serving Christianity hinder experiencing body life?

CHAPTER

2

Relational Growth through Body Life

*"We win when each member **grows in relationship** with Jesus, being, doing, thinking like Him, influencing growth and maturity in the body of Christ."*

When we think of Christian education, we tend to think of learning about God and things pertaining to Him. Cognitive learning is often the goal of Christian education. Christians desire to have an intellectual knowledge of God in Christ. The quest is to deepen themselves in the Word of God in order to master the Bible and grasp its truths for all it is worth. Although the quest to know God with the mind is admirable, it must only be a means and not the end of the pursuit. We dare not dismiss the importance of cognitive knowledge; however, we must understand that the Bible was written that we might know Jesus and not just know about Him (see John 17:3; 1 John 5:13-20). Knowing about God can simply be a religious pursuit. The religionists and the philosophers on Mars Hill simply desired to know about Jesus. Paul was attempting to introduce them to the true and living God who was and is relational (see Acts 17:16-34).

The idea of an "unknown" God is one of an impersonal God to whom we cannot relate. This is not the God of the Bible. Our God is personal and relational. Although He is above us in transcendent holiness, He is near us in His gracious presence through theophanies and ultimately through the incarnation of Christ (see John 1:14). Jesus among us is relational; the Holy Spirit dwelling in us is relational (see John 14:15-17); thus, in His plural oneness God is relational. In the mystery of oneness found in the doctrine of the Trinity, God is monotheistically presented in three distinct persons who are relational within the Trinity. This three-in-one relational God created humanity to be relational, for it was God who declared that *"it is not good that man should be alone; I will make him a helper fit for him"* (Genesis 2:18, ESV). Certainly, the "one another-ness" in the body of Christ is relational.

Christianity as Relational

Christianity is considered one of the great religions of the world. Among other great religions are Judaism, Islam, Hinduism, and Buddhism. However, it is the fact that Christianity is relational that makes it stand apart from the others. Christians follow their leader Christ in an intimate relationship, which is more profound than simply following His teachings. This type of intimacy is not found in the other religions such as Islam, Hinduism, or Buddhism. There is intimacy in Judaism, but it is not as dynamic as Christianity. The incarnation and indwelling phenomenon that is fundamental to Christianity renders it super-relational and intimate. In Christianity, there are those who are fans of Christ, but it is the true followers of Christ that are partakers of the nature of God (see 2 Peter 1:4), and possessors of the life of Christ (see John 17:20-26; 1 John 5:11-12). The exclusivity of Christianity is expressed in the New Testament's use of the preposition "in" when expressing the Christian's relationship with Christ (see 2 Corinthians 5:17; Ephesians 1:3-10; Colossians 1:27; Galatians 2:20; Romans 8:1, 9-11; Revelation 14:13).

The Christian relationship that begins in regeneration grows through sanctification. Peter admonishes the Christians to *"grow in grace and in the knowledge of our Lord and Savior Jesus Christ"* (2 Peter 3:18, NKJV). To grow in knowledge with no sense of grace is to grow unaware of the relationship with Jesus Christ as a person. Remember, the pursuit is to know Him and not merely to know about Him. If we are not careful, we can know more about Bible and be less acquainted with Christ, who is the central theme of the Bible. Living and growing in grace will help that knowledge to be more than cognitive.

Christ does not desire that we merely practice Christianity. When we as Christians become mere practitioners of Christianity, we fall into the realm of being religious. Being religious—or adhering to the laws of a particular religion (in this case Christianity)—is an attempt to live a Christian life without allowing the Holy Spirit to do His work in and through us, which is an insult to the Holy Spirit (see Acts 1:4-8; Ephesians 4:30; 5:18). Christ does not want us to attempt to live the Christian life by merely doing for God, which equates to religion. Christianity is not just the Christian doing for God; it is the Holy Spirit operating in the life of the Christian. Christianity is not duty driven; it is grace driven (see 1 Corinthians 15:10). Christianity is not a legalistic response to God; it is a love response to Him. Dynamic Christianity is not formed by an attempt to please God through the flesh; it is transforming power at work in the believer (see 2 Timothy 3:5). A Christian that is powerless is a Christian that is religious. We as Christians do drift into functioning in the flesh (see Galatians 3:3). We need the Holy Spirit operating in our lives. Attempting to be Christian without the Holy Spirit can be a form of self-righteousness.

Relational Pursuit in Sanctification

*"We win when each member grows **in relationship** with Jesus."*

Individual spiritual growth is never just personal, it is interpersonal. Personal growth is for the sake of the body. I believe that this is the thrust of the apostle Paul's win statement for the church. He wrote, *"until we all attain to the unity of the faith, and of the knowledge of the Son of God, to the mature man, to the measure of the stature which belongs to the fullness of Christ"* (Ephesians 4:13, NASB). The win is when each member seeks to grow for the sake of the whole body. We must think in terms of body life. There is a lot of solo Christianity talk in the church these days, such as: "It is my turn to receive a blessing"; "Lord, do this or that for me"; "My victory, deliverance, and prosperity are on the way." The terms used are "my" and "me", instead of "we" and "us." Although salvation is personal, solo Christianity is not God's design for His church. We are saved individually, but then immediately connected to one another in the body of Christ (see Galatians 3:26-29).

If the church is to be the fullness of Christ in the world, it is imperative that each member grows in relationship with Jesus to avoid being religious. God wants to have a relationship with us. He went walking in the Garden of Eden looking for Adam and Eve because of His personal relationship with them. God became flesh in Jesus and dwelt among us because He wanted a relationship with us. God was with us in Christ in order that He might reconcile us to Himself. One must have a relationship with God before that person can grow in the relationship. As aforementioned, one must be born of the Spirit before there can be growth in the Spirit.

More Than Anything

Spiritual growth focuses on the believer's relationship with Jesus. Biblical knowledge is a means of growing in relationship with Him, not an end. Bible teachers should be mindful of the students' relationship with Jesus as they teach. Teachers should teach the head in order to reach the heart. It is in reaching the heart that relationships are formed and developed. For this reason, I think Christian education should be viewed as discipleship, and teachers should function as disciple-makers. Teachers should seek that believers conform to the image of God's Son; this transformation happens as the believer grows in relationship with Jesus and one another.

God wants a relationship with us more than anything—not because He is lonely, but because He is relational. He is the Triune God. He is one God in three distinct persons. He is essentially relational in His being, and He created people in His image and likeness to expand His relational self reflectively. However, humanity (through Adam) went rogue on Him, and He reached out to restore the relationship with humanity (beginning with Adam). God's relational character was evident in His question to Adam in the Garden in the cool of the day when He asked: *"Adam, where are you?"* (Genesis 3:9, NKJV) The God who rested from His creative activity came out of retirement to reconcile humanity back into relationship with Himself. He entered the Garden of Eden anthropomorphically, and He entered the world anthropologically through the incarnation as He became God with us, in order to reconcile us back into relationship with Himself. God went back to work on His creation to restore the broken relationship between Himself and people. He made the first move because humanity was unable to do so. Humanity, *"dead in trespasses and sins"* (Ephesians 2:1b, NKJV) needed to be acted upon. By way of the incarnation, *"God was in Christ reconciling the world to Himself, not imputing their trespasses to them, and has committed to us the word of reconciliation"* (2 Corinthians 5:19).

In order to restore the relationship between Himself and His creation, God had to redeem us through the life-giving blood of His Son. It was a costly and painful redemption, not for us, however, but for the Father and the Son. *"For He made Him who knew no sin to be sin for us, that we might become the righteousness of God in Him"* (2 Corinthians 5:21, NKJV). To restore our relationship with God, Jesus experienced abandonment, alienation, and the agony of a sin-bearer. *"And about the ninth hour Jesus cried out with a loud voice, saying 'Eli, Eli, lama sabachthani' that is 'My God, My God, why have you forsaken Me?'"* (Matthew 27:46, NKJV) Jesus died to deliver us from the wrath of God (see Romans 1:18; John 3:36). But more than anything, Jesus died to bring us back into a relationship as sons and daughters of God.

In regeneration, we have a new nature and a right standing (justification). Through the blood of Jesus we are declared righteous, released from condemnation (see Romans 5:1; 8:1), and we become children of God (see Romans 8:14-17). Christianity is relational in that it is a Father-children relationship. Christ redeemed us in order to have a relationship with us (see Galatians 4:4-7). The reason I am so emphatic about this is since God endured all of this pain to restore the relationship with us, we certainly should pursue and cultivate our relationship with Him.

The apostle Paul's relationship with God started on the Damascus Road while Paul was traveling to Syria to do harm to the followers of the Way (Christians). It was his religious conviction that drove him to persecute those who were in right relationship with God through Christ. On that eventful day, his encounter with Jesus moved him from religion to a relationship with Christ as Lord. At the feet of Jesus, he entered into a lifelong relationship with God in Christ. All relationships with God begin at the feet of Jesus. The second stanza of the hymn, "I Surrender All," says it best:

"All to Jesus I surrender, humbly at His feet I bow;
worldly pleasures all forsaken, Take me Jesus, take me now."[8]

No one truly comes to God standing. In essence, faith in God says, "I can't; therefore, I surrender to Christ, who can." In faith, we bow at the feet of Jesus. Jesus alone can save us. Jesus is the only one qualified to save us (see Acts 4:12).

After a thirty-year relationship with Christ, the apostle Paul was still in pursuit of a deeper and closer relationship with Jesus. At the time he wrote the following passage, he was probably at the end of his life and had an insatiable desire to know Jesus:

"But what things were gain to me, these I have counted loss for Christ. Yet indeed I also count all things loss for the excellence of the knowledge of Christ

---

8 Hymn by Judson W. Van De Venter, Winfield S. Weeden

Jesus my Lord, for whom I have suffered the loss of all things, and count them as rubbish, that I may gain Christ and be found in Him, not having my own righteousness, which is from the law, but that which is through faith in Christ, the righteousness which is from God by faith; that I may know Him and the power of His resurrection, and the fellowship of His sufferings, being conformed to His death, if, by any means, I may attain to the resurrection from the dead" (Philippians 3:7-10, NKJV).

Knowing Him versus Knowing about Him

At the risk of being redundant, I am going to say more about the difference between knowing Jesus intimately and knowing Him intellectually. The Gnostics, who troubled the church in the first century with their erroneous teachings of secret knowledge that favored an impersonal Jesus, were challenged by Paul's teachings of Jesus as the God-man. Paul did not view knowledge as being for the elitist in the faith or the most biblically astute saints, but every Christian was privileged to know Jesus personally. Paul was a brilliant thinker and could be thought of as the theologian of the New Testament. He was used by the Holy Spirit to shape Christian doctrine as he himself sought to cultivate knowing Jesus relationally. He was not satisfied with his experience on the road to Damascus. He had a deep passion to know Jesus intimately. His scholarship did not render him a skeptic or cynic of Christianity. His deep knowledge of Jesus was a means of cultivating his relationship with Christ, which caused him to fall more and more in love with Christ. To Paul, the value of knowing Christ could not be compared to anything else (see Philippians 3:8). He considered all things worthless in comparison to his pursuit of his relationship with Christ. His experience of grace brought him to Peter's point to *"grow in grace and knowledge of our Lord and Savior Jesus Christ"* (2 Peter 3:18, NKJV). Paul was an exegetical genius and giant, and his grace experience led him to cultivate a love relationship with Jesus.

To know Christ in the power of His resurrection stresses the critical role of the resurrection in the life of Paul and every member of the body of Christ. The apostle saw this resurrection power as a present and continuous experience of those in right relationship with Christ. Knowing Christ in resurrection power is having and growing in the new life. This resurrection life is the life of the risen Lord. This new life is new-in-kind and shared by every member of the new body. This resurrection power brings the believer into a mystical union with Christ, a relationship with Christ that is beyond human comprehension. It starts with being crucified with Christ and ends in dynamic resurrection (see Romans 6:1-11; Galatians 2:20).

Knowing about Christ historically and biblically cannot be compared with knowing Him in the power of His resurrection (see Philippians 3:10). Through the power of the risen Christ, we have a personal experience with Him. This is the understanding in Paul's personal mission statement to know Christ in the power of His resurrection and fellowship of His sufferings (see Philippians 3:10). His personal mission was to develop a relationship with Jesus that would include having fellowship with Christ's sufferings. The new relationship in power would enable enduring the sufferings and making sense of all of it to the point of glorying in it (see Romans 5:3).

In body life, each member shares the same life (see John 17:20-26; Ephesians 4:15-16). With the physical body, the hand shares the same life as the foot; the same is true in the body of Christ. Each member of the body shares resurrection/eternal life. We are stewards of Jesus' life. The gift of eternal life is given to us by Jesus (see John 10:28) and is His life (see 1 John 5:11-12). Even natural life comes from Him, the life-giving King (see John 1:1-5). In Him is life; plants, insects, animals, and humans all find existence in Him. As God's creation, we share His life, but as members of the body of Christ, we share His life in a more intimate sense.

Each member of the body is responsible for growing in his/her relationship with Jesus, not for the sake of the individual, but for the sake of the body. The purpose of spiritual gifts in the body is to facilitate growth in the body, and of the body. Gifts are given to enable relational growth in order to build up the body in love. Growth in maturity will influence growth numerically. Incarnate growth will enhance increase. Loving and serving one another is essential to this growth. It is for the sake of the body that each member must grow in relationship with Jesus; therefore, non-growth in the body is selfishness. Body life demands that every member grows, and failure to grow causes dysfunction in the body (see Ephesians 4:15-16).

Pursuing the Relationship Has Its Perils

Having and pursuing our relationship with Christ is perilous. In fact, the presence of peril is evidence that a person is in right relationship with Him. Being related to Christ will automatically get us into trouble with the enemies of Christ. It is open season on the body of Christ, and we are not even protected, not even in a democratic nation.

"For we do not wrestle against flesh and blood, but against rulers, against the authorities, against the cosmic powers over this present darkness, against the spiritual forces of evil in the heavenly places" (Ephesians 6:12, ESV).

The enemies of Christ cannot get to Him, so they have turned their full attention on His relatives. Paul alluded to this when he wrote, *"I now rejoice in my sufferings for you, and fill up in my flesh what is lacking in the afflictions of Christ, for the sake of His body, which is the church"* (Colossians 1:24, NKJV).

Paul did not take pleasure in suffering as a masochist would. He rejoiced in his sufferings because it was confirmation that he was related to Christ. His relationship with Jesus led him to seek God's righteousness which, in turn, led to his experiencing mistreatment from the enemies of Christ. This was the plight of the early Christians. Because of their relationship with Christ, early Christians experienced great persecution. They did not coexist, or even exist in mutual tolerance, with the world. They were countercultural, and being at odds with the culture of the world was their way of life. Although Christians existed in the world, they did not belong to the world and were picked out to be picked on. Religious Christians are less likely to suffer for righteousness' sake than relational Christians.

Pursuing the Relationship Has Its Demands

Paul's pursuit of knowing Christ called for him to be *"conformed to His death"* (Philippians 3:10). Relationship with Christ will not only lead to sufferings but also to separation. When Paul speaks of death in the preceding verse, he is not suggesting that in some way Christians will experience physical crucifixion. Christ's death was sufficient. The phrase "conformed to His death" is metaphoric. Personal denial and separation is symbolic of death. Bonhoeffer wrote: "When Jesus calls a man He bids him come and die."[9] In death, one surrenders his or her life to the will of the Lord. Jesus said, *"If anyone would come after me, let him deny himself and take up his cross daily and follow me"* (Luke 9:23, ESV). The new relationship with Christ is one that demands living on the altar, separated from the world (see Romans 12:1-2), calls for practical holiness, which is a response to positional holiness (see 1 Peter 1:13-16), and calls for practicing righteousness in response to receiving Christ's righteousness (see 1 John 2:29; 3:7).

This reality is demonstrated on earth through the institution of marriage. The demand of marriage is for a man and a woman to be separated and set apart unto each other in a holy relational covenant:

"For this reason a man shall leave his father and mother and be joined to his wife, and the two shall become one flesh. So then they are no longer two

---

9   Dietrich Bonhoeffer, The Cost of Discipleship.

but one flesh. Therefore what God has joined together let not man separate" (Matthew 19:5-6, NKJV).

Marriage sets apart the couple, demanding that they forsake all others as they enter an exclusive relationship with one another. Adultery violates the requirements of this exclusive relationship. Philippians 3:7-9 sounds as if Paul were at the marriage altar repeating his vows of commitment to Christ (see above).

Does it not sound like Paul was entering into a covenant relationship with Christ? He was willing to separate, to conform to death, and to suffer loss in order to gain Christ and be found in Him. In relationships, we are called to lose self in order to enter into a new relationship of plural oneness. This is imperative in the marital relationship, and it is no wonder that many marriages do not endure when either the husband or the wife is unwilling to "lose" him- or herself for the sake of the relationship.

My advice to those desiring to get married is not to pursue marriage unless you are willing to lose yourself for the sake of the relationship. Mike Mason states the following in his book, *The Mystery of Marriage*:

"If people understood the true depth of self abnegation that marriage demands, there would perhaps be fewer weddings. For marriage, too, would be seen as a form of suicide. It would be seen not as a way of augmenting one's comfort and security in life, but rather as a way of losing one's life for the sake of Christ."[10]

Pursuing this new relationship with Christ demands prioritizing the kingdom, righteousness, and relationships (see Matthew 6:33; Luke 14:25-26; Matthew 10:37-39). The new relationship with Christ demands obedience to the will of God and walking in the way of God, according to the Word of God. The new birth ushers us into the kingdom of God where

---

10   Mike Mason, The Mystery of Marriage (Multnomah Press; Portland, Oregon, 1958), p. 137.

we are under His rule and reign. Jesus told Nicodemus that Nicodemus could not see or enter this kingdom without having this new relationship with Him (see John 3:3-5). It is a kingdom of righteousness wherein the right relationship with Christ is guided by God's standards, which are congruent with His moral nature.

Pursuing the New Relationship with Jesus Demands Love

Duty is a religious response to God. Love is a relational response to God. God demonstrated His love towards us while we were yet sinners (see Romans 5:6-11). Several passages of Scripture remind us that Christianity is not driven by fear, but motivated by love (see John 14:15, 21, 23; 15:10; 1 John 2:3; 5:3; 2 John 6). As Christians, our willingness to give, serve, sacrifice, submit, suffer, devote, discipline, practice, perform, worship, witness, work, forgive, forebear, preach, teach, pray, sing, and minister is simply a response to our love relationship with God through Christ in the power of the Holy Spirit (see Romans 5:5).

That we cannot be separated from God's love is indicative of a relational God (see Romans 8:31-39). God is eternally in love with us. To grow in relationship with Jesus is to grow in love with Him. Before we entered our mutual love affair with God, we were the recipients of love demonstrated through grace (see Romans 5:8). The reason why God hates divorce, especially among Christians, is because it is inconsistent with His permanent love for us. One of the purposes in Christian marriage is to reflect the truth of God's relationship with those who belong to Him.

God's love for us is our impetus for loving one another in the body of Christ. The vertical relationship must precede the horizontal relationship, making it impossible to love God and hate a fellow member of the body of Christ (see 1 John 2:11; 3:17-18; 4:7-12, 20). The loving fellowship (the church) is designed so that the win is experienced within loving relationships. When Christians use their spiritual gifts in the context of loving one another as God in Christ has loved us, there will be healthy body life. There will be no sense of inferiority or superiority in the body of Christ where members are engaged in attempting to out-love each other. When members are determined to achieve the win for the sake of the whole body of Christ, each member will grow in relationship with Jesus and each other. Authentic relationships develop an unconditional and sacrificial love. The love of God was demonstrated through the church of Thessalonica. The apostle Paul commended them when he wrote:

"We are bound to thank God always for you brethren, as it is fitting, because your faith grows exceedingly, and the love of every one of you all abounds towards each other" (2 Thessalonians 1:3, NKJV).

Pursuing our relationship with Jesus is both personal and interpersonal, and it includes growing in relationship with one another in the body of Christ. The indispensable union that every believer enters through Spirit baptism makes personal spiritual growth essential to the health of the body of Christ. Growing in relationship with Jesus will not be authentic unless there is interrelational growth. Warren Wiersbe states, *"The fact that Christians love one another is evidence of their fellowship with God and their sonship from God, and it is also evidence that they know God."*[11] God will not allow us to grow close to Him without growing close to one another in the body of Christ (see Matthew 5:23, 24; 1 Peter 3:7).

When sin infiltrates the fellowship, the whole body of Christ is affected, and discipline must ensue. The apostle Paul confronted the Corinthian church for their refusal to discipline a brother because of his sin, which harmed the church's witness (see 1 Corinthians 5:1-13). There are times when sin in the church needs to be exposed. When a member of the body continues in sin and refuses to repent, that person must be exposed, just as the prophet Nathan did with David and his sin in 2 Samuel 12:1-15.

---

11   Warren Wiersbe, The Bible Exposition Commentary (Vol. 2) (Chariot Victor Publishing, Colorado Springs, 1989), p. 516.

However, there are occasions when the sins of a brother or sister need covering (see Proverbs 10:12; 1 Peter 4:8; James 5:20).

When a brother or sister has sinned and is repentant, there is no need to expose that sin. The sin of that remorseful saint is to be covered (or forgiven), an act that follows the example of our loving Father who has taken away our sins (see Hebrews 9:26). Whether a church's discipline involves exposing a sin or covering a sin, it is a demonstration of love. Once a person becomes a member of the body, he or she cannot sin apart from the body. There is no such thing as a private life independent of the body. As stated earlier, sin committed by a member of the body of believers affects the whole body, no matter if the sin is committed publicly or privately. Either way, a healthy church knows when the sin needs to be covered or when it needs to be exposed.

Walking with God

Walking with God is how Christians pursue a relationship with Him. Both Noah and Enoch were known for walking with God (see Genesis 5:24; 6:9). I believe that it was Noah's walk more than his work that resulted in his family's entering the ark. Enoch was privileged to escape death when the Lord took him home.

The apostle Paul welcomed death so he could be with the Lord (see Philippians 1:21-24). Working for God is not a substitute for walking with God. Christian service requires both working for God and walking with God. However, working for God is not to take priority over walking with God, and if it does the service becomes ineffective. Pursuing the relationship with God takes precedence in order that service is not done in the flesh, which is what occurs when the relationship with God is neglected. The busyness of ministry can deter our walk with God. If we are not careful, even Bible study can be all about filling the head and not the heart. Satan will use good things to keep us from walking with God, and if he causes us to drift from our "first love" (see Revelation 2:4), we can lose our passion, purpose, and power. If we are to faithfully walk with the Lord, we must have more than a crush on the Christ; we must have a robust romance with the Redeemer. Walking with the Lord must become more than an event.

Our quiet time does not capture the full meaning of what it really means to walk with the Lord. Walking with the Lord is a lifestyle, not simply just a meeting. Walking with the Lord is a marital relationship; however, it is more intimate than a marriage between a man and a woman. Marriage may be reflective of the one-flesh relationship, but our relationship with Jesus is a mysterious intimacy (see John 17:20-26; Colossians 1:27; 2 Corinthians 5:17). In a Christian marriage, the couple becomes a marital person (see Ephesians 5:28-33), but the intimacy is not as dynamic and permanent as our relationship with Christ (see Romans 8:35-39). More than in reverence to God, we live in relationship with Him (see Colossians 3:1-4).

To cultivate the relationship, the Word of God must be at home in us (see Colossians 3:16). We must meditate on the Word day and night (see Psalm 1:2). We cannot grow in relationship with Jesus unless the Word of God is internalized (see Psalm 119:11). Praying three times a day like Daniel is good, but praying without ceasing is better (see Ephesians 6:17-20). A life of prayer is a life of submission and dependence on God (see Romans 12:12; Philippians 4:6; 1 Thessalonians 5:17). Walking in the Spirit is essential to cultivating your relationship with Jesus (see Galatians 5:16). Giving God uninterrupted time in the morning or the evening is a good practice, but taking advantage of the Spirit's indwelling presence and relating to Him throughout the day is far better.

In this new age of telecommunications advances, people are able to communicate by sending and receiving text messages just about anytime and anywhere. Because of the spiritual nature of our relationship with God in Christ, it is also possible for us to communicate with Him by praying in our spirit throughout the day no matter where we are (see 1 Corinthians 14:15). We have the capacity to cultivate and develop our relationship with God in Christ throughout the day by means of Scripture memorization, praying in the Spirit, and meditation. This mysteriously and miraculously intimate relationship with Jesus is not limited to times and places. The omnipresence of God is realized in the believer in a personal, permanent, purposeful, and powerful sense. Sin may keep us from realizing His presence (see 1 John 1:5-10), but nothing can separate us from this love relationship (see Romans 8:31-39).

An Authentic Intimacy with God in Christ Is Infectious

The greatest commandment is love:

"Jesus said to him, 'You shall love the Lord your God with all your heart, with all your soul, and with all your mind. This is the first and greatest commandment. And the second is like it: 'You shall love your neighbor as yourself.' On these two commandments hang all the Law and the Prophets" (Matthew 22:37-40, NKJV).

The two commandments are progressive: Loving God affects loving others. Although it is commanded, it is also contagious. True intimacy with God is infectious. We are confronted with the following question: Is it possible to have a robust relationship with the Redeemer and at the same time have a weak, infirmed relationship with a spouse, siblings, and other saints? In other words, is it possible to have a good relationship with God and a bad relationship with others? Plainly speaking, can you be engaged in pursuing your relationship with God and at the same time have a poisonous relationship with others? The answer is that one cannot adequately grow in their relationship with Jesus and be engaged in a bad relationship with others. Growing in relationship with Jesus and being faithful to Him will enhance your horizontal relationships and enable you to be faithful in them, especially in the marital relationship (see 1 John 4:20-21, NKJV).

The bottom line is if there are problems on the horizontal level, more likely than not something is not right on the vertical level. Attempting to cultivate a relationship with Jesus without reconciliation on the horizontal level is living in self-deception (see Matthew 5:21-26). You and I cannot go forward with God until we go back and face the sins that have disconnected us from others. In the penitential Psalms 6, 32, 38, 51, 102, 130, and 143, we sense David's contrite spirit after trespassing upon the marriage and life of Uriah. His violation of Uriah's marriage interrupted his relationship with God (see Psalm 51:8-13, NKJV). Because of David's sin, Israel's enemies blasphemed the Lord (see 2 Samuel 12:14, ASV). At that point in David's life, his relationship with the Lord was not infectious but infamous.

There is power in an intimate relationship with Jesus. It is hard to argue with someone who has an obvious relationship with Him. When Christianity flows from an authentic relationship, it is infectious. Those outside of Christ are more apt to ask questions concerning the hope that is evident in contagious Christianity (see 1 Peter 3:13-17). A contagious church is a church where the love of Christ is spread abroad in the hearts of each member of the body of Christ (see John 13:35; 1 Corinthians 13). The most effective witness is when a Christian and the church demonstrate an authentic love for Christ and one another in the body. A love that goes up to God and out towards one another will become an instrument that the Spirit can use to draw all people unto Christ. I will more comprehensively address this later in the book.

Think It Through

1. Why is the term "discipleship" more relational than "Christian education"?

2. What makes Christianity more relational than religion?

3. What should be the aim of cognitive learning?

4. Why is personal spiritual growth necessary for the health of the body of Christ?

5. How is God relational within Himself?

6. In what way or ways is our relationship with Christ congruent with sufferings and death?

7. What does it mean to pursue your relationship with Jesus, and what are the benefits?

8. Why is it inconsistent to grow close to Christ and not close to other Christians in the body of Christ?

9. Why is it more important to cultivate one's walk with Jesus than one's work for Him?

10. Why is an intimate relationship with Jesus infectious?

CHAPTER

3

Becoming like Jesus

*"We win when each member grows in relationship with Jesus, **being,** doing, thinking like Him, influencing growth and maturity in the body of Christ."*

Someone once said, "Association brings about assimilation." The title "Christian" was given to followers of Christ because they demonstrated His character, not simply because they followed His teachings (see Acts 11:26). It is significant that the name "Christian" was not given by friends of Christ but by foes of Christ.

Clarifying Our Destination

Our destination as Christians has been more geographical than one of glorification. Most Christians long to make heaven their destination and home. Some Christians even speak of striving to make heaven their home as if it depended upon their effort. The win for them is to cross the heavenly goal line. To quote a line from an old Negro spiritual: *"On Jordan's stormy banks I stand and cast a wishful eye."* Certainly, to be with Jesus is our heavenly hope, but to be like Him is our glorious hope. Hope is the certainty of a reality not yet experienced. Heaven is a certainty not yet experienced, but glorification is a certainty not completely experienced (see 2 Corinthians 3:18; 1 John 3:1-3).

Salvation begins with regeneration, continues in sanctification, and consummates in glorification. Somehow we have lost sight of the doctrine of glorification. Paul gives us the process of salvation when he wrote:

"For whom He foreknew, He also predestined to be conformed to the image of His Son, that He might be the firstborn among many brethren. Moreover

whom He predestined, these He called; whom He called, these He also justified, and whom He justified these He also glorified" (Romans 8:29-30, NKJV).

Growing in relationship with Jesus is growing towards being like Jesus. To know Jesus cognitively is only a means of being conformed into His image. Therefore, the destination for the Christian is being conformed to His image. The believer's destination is to be like Him and not merely be with Him.

Adam and Eve's Desire and Our Destiny

The tempter said to Eve, *"For God knows that in the day you eat of it your eyes will be opened, and you will be like God, knowing good and evil"* (Genesis 3:5, NKJV). Why did the fall have to occur when all Adam and Eve wanted was to be like God? If our destination is to be conformed to the image of God's Son, what is wrong with our primal parents' quest to be like God? The answer is because Adam and Eve were created in God's image and likeness, but they wanted more; they wished to be gods. Satan was jealous of the fact that humankind was made a little lower than the angels (see Psalm 8:4-5), so in his fateful fallen state, he wanted company. He knew what happened to him when he attempted to be more than he was created to be (see Isaiah 14:12-15).

Let me attempt to illustrate that which is beyond my comprehension: God the Father is the mass of the sun; God the Son is the brightness of the glory of the sun, God the Holy Spirit is the warmth of the sun, the angels are the stars, and humankind is the moon. The stars are lesser lights and the moon is reflective light. Satan and the angels who followed him desired to be the greater lights, and Adam and Eve desired to be more than reflective lights. Sadly, this insidious desire to be gods is still among us. We hear of it in Mormonism as well as in some erroneous Christian teachings, teachings wherein people can evolve towards divinity.

From Glory to Gloom

In Genesis 1:31, God declared that all He had created was good, including human beings, whom He made in His image to be a reflection of His image, likeness, and glory. Although the heavens declare God's glory, humanity was created to reflect God's glory in a personal way, but no one shares God's glory. Glory belongs to Him alone (see Isaiah 48:11; Matthew 6:13). Humanity was created also to reflect what is true of God, not just through proclamation, but through ontology as well.

The Fall (of humanity) occurred and sin was ushered in, and it was at this point that humans went from reflective glory to regressive gloom (see Romans 1:16-32). Humanity not only lost Paradise, but its personhood was severely impaired. Paul said, *"In sin, man fell short of the glory of God"* (Romans 3:23, NKJV). Humanity fell short of his ought-ness and became less than what God created them to be. Therefore, sin is not the activity of a human being, but rather a subhuman being. When we sin, we are not being human, and to say that we sin because "we are only human" is a false statement, and it places blame on the Creator and testifies falsely about God. Sin is against the very nature of God. Sin is not merely telling lies, it is being a lie. Coming short of God's glory is coming short of the truth about who God is. King David's confession of his sins denotes how he saw his sin as primarily being committed against who God is and not merely against what God said (see Psalm 51:3-4). Sin is anti-God, anti-human, and anti-cosmos (see Romans 8:22-23).

Human Recovery

Desiring that humans recover from the Fall (of humanity), God had to become like us in order for us once again to become like Him. Therefore, the incarnation of God was vital for human recovery. Although salvation is deliverance from the wrath of God (see John 3:36; 5:24; Romans 1:18; 8:1), salvation was also vital for human recovery. By human recovery, I do not infer reformation, but the regenerative work of the Holy Spirit operative in the new person (see John 3:5-8). Through salvation humankind became a new creation, and what was lost in the first Adam was restored through the reconciling work of the Second Adam, Jesus Christ. What God intended in Adam and Eve's humanity was made possible through the incarnation, crucifixion, and resurrection of Jesus. The resurrection of the body signifies human recovery (see 1 Corinthians 15). Jesus' resurrection is the first fruit of the resurrection that we will experience someday. Being like Jesus has a human component to it. Jesus is authentically Man and has a resurrected body in heaven, and one day we will be like Him.

"Behold what manner of love the Father has bestowed on us, that we should be called children of God! Therefore the world does not know us, because it did not know Him. Beloved, now we are children of God; and it has not yet been revealed what we shall be, but we know that when He is revealed, we shall be like Him, for we shall see Him as He is" (1 John 3:1-2, NKJV).

From Gloom to Glory

Being like Jesus is not synonymous with acting like Jesus. Christians are not actors playing a role, nor are we merely imitating Christ. Our relationship with Jesus is not only a partnership, but we actually become partakers of God's divine nature as well (see 2 Peter 1:4). Our relationship is organic as we possess the life of Christ (see Colossians 3:3-4; 1 John 5:11-13). We grow in relationship with Jesus and we are becoming who we are in Him. Discipleship is more than just Christian education. It is developing the Jesus-nature which is implanted at regeneration by the Holy Spirit (see John 3:8), and through the regenerating, sanctifying relationship with Jesus, we are being conformed into His image (see Romans 8:29). The transformation is like the metamorphosis of a caterpillar into a butterfly. It is a glorious change from gloom to glory (see 2 Corinthians 3:18), shepherding us back to glory is God's purpose in salvation.

Satan is mad as hell perhaps because God did not send a Savior for him and his fallen angels, and because human recovery is in God's salvific plan, Satan's jealousy of humans has escalated:

"But we are bound to give thanks to God always for you, brethren beloved by the Lord, because God from the beginning chose you for salvation through sanctification by the Spirit and belief in the truth, to which He called you by our gospel, for the obtaining of the glory of our Lord Jesus Christ" (2 Thessalonians 2:13-14, NKJV).

What marvelous words of comfort and assurance for the Thessalonians and for us. Our God is going to see the process all the way through. We will return to this truth later in this book.

Being conformed into the image of Jesus is returning to authentic humanity, which is what was lost in the first Adam but gained in the Second Adam. Our being like Jesus is in accordance with His humanity, not His deity. Remember, in sin humanity is subhuman and only in the Man Jesus are we restored to God's original intention for humanity. Jesus is authentically human, and outside of Him we are inauthentically human. Going back to glory means that humanity is returning to its creative purpose, and that is to reflect the image of God through his humanity (see Colossians 3:10).

The incarnation and resurrection of Jesus Christ are pivotal to human recovery. The Man Jesus and the bodily resurrection of Jesus speak volumes to salvation as human recovery. Jesus did not just appear to be human. He was fully human. However, His sinless humanity declares that He is authentic humanity. To substitute for people's sins, Jesus had to be the real deal and at the same time be without sin (see 2 Corinthians 5:21). Then bodily resurrection had to be just as real. Salvation is not complete until the believer experiences bodily resurrection. In heaven with Jesus, we will be human beings with resurrected bodies (see 1 Corinthians 15:35-49;

1 Thessalonians 4:13-18). Yes! Being like Jesus is being humanly like Him.

To be like Jesus is to think in terms of His humanity. In His humanity, He is the exactness of the glory of the Father (see Hebrews 1:3). Our likeness is reflective. Jesus is the revelation of God. He discloses Him perfectly. He is the Light of the world, and we are mere lights in the world. Through the incarnation, Jesus discloses the Father and defines authentic humanity. In this One Person, we have the God-man. He is both the Son of God and the Son of Man. Although this truth of Scripture is incomprehensible—the joining of two natures in one person—it is a divine mystery realized only in Jesus. Mysteriously, in Jesus is the finite and infinite. They are not commingled in Him.

It is because of this mystery of the two natures in Jesus of Nazareth that we are awarded the capacity to be transformed into the same image from glory to glory (see 2 Corinthians 3:18, NKJV). Again, by "the same image" I mean full humanity—true of Jesus, and becoming true of us. When speaking of Jesus as all human and all God, in the incarnation He was among us yet above us, humanly speaking. Also, He was like us humanly but at the same time so much unlike us (see Philippians 2:7; 2 Corinthians 5:21). As a witness, Jesus tells the truth about God and people. For us to be like Him, Jesus had to become like us. And at the same time, He had to be unlike us in order to redeem us from the curse of the Law, which uncovered our spoiled humanity (see Galatians 3:13; 4:4-7). I have sought to refer to the image of God in ontological terms rather than in functional terms. Certainly, the image of God must not be viewed as physical, as some have attempted to view it. The functional sense, as it relates to self-consciousness, self-determination, and moral consciousness, encompasses the properties of all humanity, saints and sinners alike, although impaired by sin. The image in humanity separates humankind from all other creatures and life forms. Human value is deeply rooted in image-bearing and belonging to the one whose image humanity reflects (see Genesis 9:6).

I do not believe that the doctrine of total depravity removes the image of God in people. However, the human image of God is damaged and can be restored only in Christ. The image of God is distorted from God's (*telos*) intended purpose for humanity. All people possess the image of God, but not His life. Like the heavens declare the glory of God (see Psalm 19:1; Acts 14:17), humankind declares His glory in that he is a rational, conscious, creature with his own volition. If humanity does not declare the glory of God, then he is the glory. There is anthropological agreement for the existence of God in that humanity's presence on an orderly designed planet declares super-personal intelligence. Humanity is because God is. Without the life of God, people cannot be conformed towards the full image of God. The natural image must experience the supernatural image that is realized only in a relationship with Jesus (see Romans 8:28-30).

Sinners cannot grow towards being like Jesus without experiencing the new birth. They may possess noble, moral, ethical, and religious character, but without a new or changed nature God's image in people will remain impaired, distorted, and incomplete. In this tolerant age, it is difficult to say that only a relationship with and through Jesus Christ, who is the complete revelation of the image of God, can remove a person's impairment, distortion, and incompleteness. The image of God in people can only be fully restored by becoming like Jesus. The aim of Christian education or discipleship should not be to attain Bible knowledge, but the aim should be to become like Jesus. The purpose of preaching and teaching should always be to communicate the Word of God to the hearer for transformation, and not merely for information. We preach and teach in order that the Word will become flesh in the hearer. In other words, the Word must be communicated so that the believer might become who they are in Christ Jesus. Unfortunately, so much of the preaching and teaching of today is done with the goal of making believers happy instead of holy. Preachers and teachers are more concerned with the comfort of their hearers rather than their conformation to the image of God's Son. Ray Stedman made a profound statement when he wrote:

"God's first concern is not what the church does; it is what the church is. Being must always precede doing, for what we do will be according to what we are. To understand the moral character of God's people is a primary essential in understanding the nature of the church. As Christians we are to be a moral example to the world, reflecting the character of Jesus Christ."[12]

Think It Through

1. *After reading this chapter, how do you view your destination and destiny?*

2. *Why is salvation about human recovery?*

3. *In what sense are we to be like Jesus?*

4. *What was wrong with Adam and Eve's desire to be like God, in light of our destiny to be like Christ?*

5. *How does Jesus' bodily resurrection dignify humanity?*

6. *If saints and sinners both bear the image of God, why are Christians being conformed to Christ's image?*

7. *Why is the incarnation vital to human recovery?*

---

12   Ray C. Stedman, Body Life (G. L. Publishers, Glendale, California, 1972), p.13.

CHAPTER

4

Doing like Jesus

*"We win when each member grows in relationship with Jesus, being, **doing**, thinking like Him, influencing growth and maturity in the body of Christ."*

We are human *beings* before we are humans *doing*. What we do for God is only acceptable if it flows from who we are in Christ. The United States of America has been known as a Christian nation. This is more in name than in nature. Christian character and Christ-like "doings" can be exhibited by Christians and non-Christians alike. Mahatma Gandhi expressed Christian character. He could have been labeled a Hindu Christian because he embraced the teachings of Jesus as found in the Sermon on the Mount. In a sense, Gandhi's focus on truth and love in the context of nonviolence made him a pragmatic Christian. Jesus was also about truth and love. However, Jesus was the epitome of veracity and the supreme demonstration of God's redemptive love. Gandhi represents many who practice Christianity without being a Christian. There is a difference between being a Christian in name than being a Christian in nature. The Creator created us to be productive. As Christians, our actions are to flow from our being like Jesus. Our worth must first be realized on the being level and then on the doing level. Performance and position must not eclipse personhood. Who we are should be paramount, not what we do. Our craft and credentials must never supersede character. Who a person is more important than what a person does. Have you noticed that most conversations with strangers start by people asking, "What do you do?" Who we are is often measured by what we do. Performance seems to be more important than personhood. The impetus of divorce in the church—and in society in general—can be traced to what the persons do and not who the persons are. Failure to take the time to discover to whom you are getting married often leads to the demise of the marital relationship. Losing sight of the relational aspect of Christianity results in it drifting into a religion of doing. The apostle James uses the term "religion" when referring to Christian duty in his practical letter to those of the dispersion (see James 1:26, 27). Although the term "religion" rarely occurs in the New Testament, there is a religious aspect to our relationship with Jesus.

To do like Jesus is very important. Christianity must be practiced. We should not think in terms of being *versus* doing; rather we should think being *and* doing. We see this dichotomy in Mary and Martha, the sisters of Lazarus, where Mary was in the presence of Jesus cultivating her relationship with Him while Martha was engaged in service. Both are necessary, but doing ought to flow from the relationship. Serving is doing like Jesus; the truth is Jesus Himself came to serve (see Matthew 20:28). However, to use works as a gauge of our being is the same as trying to work to be saved (see Titus 3:5). We are not Christians by doing, but rather through being like Jesus. It is not our works that brings about our salvation, but rather it is the completed work of Jesus on Calvary that accomplished our salvation. Therefore, there is nothing left for us to do for our salvation; Christ did all that is needed for us to be saved. Salvation is a matter of grace through faith, which alleviates all human effort so no one can boast. Paul, who came out of a religion and into a glorious relationship with Christ said, *"I do not frustrate the grace of God: for if righteousness comes by the law, then Christ died in vain"* (Galatians 2:21, KJV). Because of the grace of God, Christians do not work to be saved; neither do we work to remain saved. However, we are God's precious product enabled by the Holy Spirit to perform good works (see Ephesians 2:10; Matthew 5:16; 2 Corinthians 9:8). It is worth noting here that in Christianity good works are always a means of pointing people to Christ so that they can know Him personally (see 1 Peter 2:11-12).

Greater Works

When Jesus promised that the apostles would do greater works, He did not mean that the substance and essence of their works would be greater than His (see John 14:12-21). The extent of the apostles' works would be greater, not the essence of their works. In other words, the apostles would do more in quantity, not in quality. The rationality for the quantity of their work would be the indwelling presence and power of the Holy Spirit (see 1 John 4:4; Philippians 2:13; Hebrews 13:21; 1 Corinthians 15:10). Jesus' absence on earth would necessitate the coming of the Other Comforter (the Holy Spirit) (see John 16:7). It sounds like Jesus was saying that His purpose in the apostles would not be accomplished if He remained in the world. He must go to the Father so the Holy Spirit could come to empower them to do the greater works.

Neither the apostles nor the church can supersede the work of Christ in the world. His creative work and redemptive work are unparalleled. On Calvary, Jesus finished His redemptive work. In securing human redemption, Jesus made possible the redemption of creation (see Romans 8:19-25). The apostles and the church will reach the world with the Gospel of redemption (see Matthew 28:19-20). The works of the apostles of Christ demonstrated through the sign-gifts that were performed by them to authenticate their message and apostleship (see 2 Corinthians 12:12). These gifted men were the foundation and Jesus was the chief cornerstone (see Ephesians 2:20), and no leader can deviate from their works (see 1 Corinthians 3:11). Christ the Lord of the church does not need His church laying a different foundation. His church is to build upon the foundation that is already laid, which is Him alone. I am strongly suggesting that the greater works are not the performance of sign-gifts done by members of the superstructure of the body of Christ. However, in many Christian circles Christians desire to see and do signs and wonders instead of being signs and wonders. The church is not to perform signs and wonders, but she is to be signs and wonders (see Ephesians 2:10).

If doing like Jesus is to be authentic, the Christian church must understand *"for it is God who works in you both to will and to do for His good pleasure"* (Philippians 2:13, NKJV). Doing good works as Christians is only acceptable to God when He is the object and source of the work (see Matthew 5:16). In that day when our works are judged, the focus will not be so much on what we did as much as it will be on why we did. Specifically, Christ will judge our motives, and it is only if our works were motivated by love will they be deemed pure. Works motivated by love comes from the realization that God desires to work through us rather than our having to work for Him. So what did Jesus do that we should emulate? He worked the works of the Father who sent Him into the world. So we must work the works of Christ who sent us into the world (see John 9:4; 20:21). What is the work that we are to continue to do? Jesus came preaching, teaching, and healing. His main focus was to seek and to save the lost (see Luke 19:10). The apostle Paul exclaimed that the church was to involve herself in the *"word and ministry of reconciliation"* (2 Corinthians 5:17-21).

Therefore, I suggest that our main duty as a congregation of the church of Jesus Christ be the work of reconciliation, allowing God to work through us to reconcile sinners back to Himself. Good works are not godly if reconciliation is not the end product. We will return to the ministry of the Christian church later in this book.

Submitting

To submit means to yield to the power or authority of another. Jesus lived a submissive life. He placed Himself under the authority and will of the Father. Although He had every right to claim His equality with the Father, He operated in subjection to Him. Paul stressed this in the Kenosis Christology (see Philippians 2:5-8). Doing like Jesus requires us as Christians to have the same mindset that Jesus had. He lived to please the Father who sent Him into the world. He did nothing without this insatiable desire to please Him (see John 8:28, 29). These expressions of humility cause many to miss His divinity that was cloaked in His humanity. Jesus downplayed His equality with the Father by being submissive to Him to the point of His seeming to be unequal with the Father. Since Jesus set the example in His condescension, certainly those of us in relationship with Jesus, being like Him, ought to do like Jesus did and live submissive lives. We are to live our lives controlled by a "your will be done, not mine" kind of life. We are definitely unequal to the Father, and to do less than submit to the Father is unthinkable and unthankful. Again, Jesus is our perfect example of living a life submitting to the will of the Father. In the Garden of Gethsemane, unlike what happened in the Garden of Eden, Jesus, the Second Adam, won His struggle against self-will. *"Father, if Thou are willing, remove this cup from Me; yet not My will, but Thine be done"* (Luke 22:42, NKJV). If we seek the will of God, we will not need to seek His forgiveness as much; but unfortunately, it appears that we would rather seek His forgiveness more than His will.

The biblical principle of submission starts on the vertical level and moves to the horizontal. Submission to God will lead to submission to one another. Self-abnegation does not stop with the God-man relationship, but it continues with the man-man relationship. In the body of Christ, there is to be mutual submission demonstrated in Christian marriage (see Ephesians 5:21-33). Paul states in Philippians 2:3-4 that we are to *"do nothing from selfishness or empty conceit, but with humility of mind let each of you regard one another as more important than himself; do not merely look out for your own personal interest, but also for the interest of others."*

Serving

It is God's will that we serve one another. Love is doing, and serving is an expression of love. Serving flows from the love of God in the believer's new nature, making it first a matter of being like Jesus (see Romans 5:5). To have Jesus' nature is to have the capacity to love others unconditionally. Loving like God loves is not merely emulating Him; it is essentially being like Him (see 1 John 3:13-24; 4:15-21; 5:1-3). We are most like Jesus when we take a towel and serve one another. Jesus came down to earth to serve and to give His life as a ransom for many (see Matthew 20:26-28). He was equal with the Father but came down to the human level as a servant, not a king. He took a servant's towel, not a sovereign's title. He washed the disciples' feet, and in so doing He modeled the role and disposition of a servant, and it is His will that we do likewise (see John 13:4-16). Not doing like Jesus is reflective of not being like Him. However, simply doing like Jesus is not what makes us Christian. Christian-like "doings" and "dogmas" do not render one a Christian (see Matthew 7:21-23; John 2:23-25). We are essentially Christians because of the new birth; Christ is in us (see 2 Corinthians 13:5; John 3:3-8; 2 Corinthians 5:17; Colossians 1:27). Loving and serving one another is a response of experiencing the love of the Servant Christ in salvation, and we serve one another by being and doing like Jesus.

Growing in relationship with Him is a means of serving in the body of Christ. When we relate to one another with an awareness of grace and interdependence, it is an act of love and service. Gene Getz said it best: *"To be a servant to others, we must first of all be a servant of righteousness."*[13] When we think of serving others, we think of acts of physical, material, or verbal

---

13   Gene A. Getz, Serving One Another (Victor Books, Wheaton, Illinois, 1984), p. 51.

expressions of kindness (see Ephesians 4:30-32; James 2:14-16). But we overlook the fact that when each member grows in relationship with Jesus, we are serving one another. It is a selfish member who refuses or neglects to pursue his or her relationship with Jesus. Each member in the body of Christ is related to Christ and to one another. Christ has so designed the church that we are interdependent and indispensably related. Growing spiritually is an act of loving one another and building up one another. So when we do not grow spiritually, the building up of one another is impaired.

Love demands that we as servants be inconvenienced as we invest into the lives of others in the body of Christ. Jesus sets the example in 2 Corinthians 8:9, and in Philippians 2:1-8 Paul challenges saints to have the same servant mindset as that of Jesus. As servants, we have the nature of Jesus and the mind of Jesus the Servant and, since we are His servants, we are to act like it. Humility characterizes servants, and there is no room in the life of servants for pride and selfishness. Servant members are enabled to serve one another in the body of Christ by the fruit and gifts of the Spirit. The fruit of Spirit have to do with being like Jesus (see Galatians 5:22-26), and the Gifts of the Spirit are for doing like Jesus (see Romans 12:3-13; 1 Corinthians 12:4-26; Ephesians 4:7-16). In the Corinthian church the gifts were misused, causing the body to malfunction. In 1 Corinthians 13, Paul called for the church to function with their gifts in the context of serving one another in love.

We are in a time where people are fascinated with titles: senior pastor, doctor, reverend, bishop, apostle, prelate, elder, and so forth. However, few people would prefer to claim the title of servant. Jesus said that worldly people like titles. His disciples wanted special recognition and special seats, but Jesus said, *"It is not so among you, but whosoever wishes to become great among you shall be your servant, and whoever wishes to be first among you shall be your slave; just as the Son of Man did not come to be served, but to serve, and to give His life a ransom for many"* (Matthew 20:26-28 NASB).

Years ago, Bill Hybels and Ron Wilkins coauthored the book, *Descending into Greatness*, a title that I found intriguing. Greatness as characterized by the world is contradictory to greatness as characterized by Jesus. Jesus said the journey towards greatness involves a downward spiral, going from servant to slave. Serving others is the path to greatness. Being under and not over is Christ's definition of greatness. Serving as opposed to being served is the true measure of greatness. What a contradistinction and witness to the worldview of things! By becoming a servant Himself, Jesus the Sovereign taught us how to serve. Jesus said, *"If anyone wishes to come after Me, let him deny himself, and take up his cross, and follow Me. For whoever wishes to save his life shall lose it; but whoever loses his life for My sake shall find it"* (Matthew 16:24-25, NASB).

Jesus served as preacher, teacher, healer, and Savior. It is clear in Scripture that Jesus came preaching, teaching, and healing (see Matthew 4:23-25; 9:35). But He primarily came to die for sinners (see 1 Timothy 1:12-15). Therefore, Jesus served us best not by His Sermon on the Mount, not by His healing ministry in Capernaum, not by His teaching ministry in the synagogue and by the seashore, not by the miracles He performed in Galilee and elsewhere, but Jesus served us best by His substitutionary death on the cross at Calvary. As we serve like Jesus in the ministries of preaching, teaching, and healing, we dare not lose sight of the importance of the cross, our engagement in the ministry, and the word of reconciliation (see 2 Corinthians 5:18-21). If the Master's manifesto (found in Luke 4:16-19) were viewed in the social, political, and economic realms, Jesus would be considered to be like most politicians who are big on promises but small on delivery. Certainly, Jesus was against sin in all of its social, political, and economic expressions, then as well as now. Jesus' manifesto focused, however, more on sin expressed through social ills and was aimed at causes not effects. Jesus came through a condemned world on His way to Calvary to save such a world (see John 3:16-21). The manifesto was more about Jesus than it was about the people. He was announcing that the

Messiah was here. His doings among them would signal His authenticity. But because it was not the social action they anticipated, the people as well as John the Baptist questioned whether or not Jesus was the promised one (see John 1:11; Luke 7:19-20). They rejected Jesus and His mission. Today there are those who wish to redefine Jesus and His mission; however, in doing so they are not doing like Jesus.

As servants, we are stewards of the Gospel ministry. Not only must preachers preach, but the congregation must preach as well (see Acts 8:4). We are all to proclaim the Gospel through preaching, through evangelism, and through witnessing. We serve in and through the body of Christ and in the world. Our service in the world is as ambassadors for Christ (see 2 Corinthians 5:20). He makes His appeal through us to a world in need of reconciliation. Christ made reconciliation possible and gave us the responsibility as His servants and stewards of the Gospel to share the Good News with those in the world who are separated from God. Jesus came into the world to atone for the sins of the world in order that the world could experience "at-one-ment" with a holy and righteous God. We remain in the world as His ambassadors to implore sinners to be reconciled to God. As servants of Christ, engaging in discipleship is doing like Jesus. The Bible does not give us a definitive definition of discipleship, but Jesus modeled it. Jesus related, revealed, and reproduced disciples. Therefore, a disciple is an obedient follower of Christ, relating, reflecting, and reproducing disciples. The church is called to make, mark, mature, and multiply disciples. The main component in the Great Commission is teaching (see Matthew 28:19, 20). To do like Jesus is to be a church that teaches disciples to be obedient followers of Christ. Evidence of salvation is love-obedience (see 1 John 4:7-12). We will return to this subject later in this discipline.

Jesus was compassionate, and as His servants we do like Him when we are compassionate. We are like Jesus when we have compassion for suffering humanity. A church devoid of compassion and mercy is not a church that is serving the Lord. The word and ministry of reconciliation is hindered where there is no compassion for the lost. One way that Jesus showed His compassion was through healing. His power to heal authenticated His ministry and His mercy. Many people in need of healing sought out Jesus, and Jesus met their needs. His miracles of healing were signs that pointed beyond the miracles themselves. The church was not commissioned to establish healing ministries. The apostles were sent to heal (see Matthew 10:1-8), but not the Lord's church. The gift of healing found in the early church was primarily done by the apostles and their associates. Healings were a part of the signs and wonders performed by the apostles (see 2 Corinthians 12:12). It authenticated the message of these men who were the foundation of the church (see Ephesians 2:20). They were not healers; they were instruments used by God as He performed the miracles of healing through them. When it comes to healings and miracles, we cannot do like Jesus nor like His apostles and prophets. Our main focus with regard to healing is not to be on developing a healing ministry but on having compassion for a sin-sick world. This is not to say that we should be unconcerned about those who are physically, emotionally, and mentally sick. We are instructed to pray for the sick (see James 5:14, 15), which is demonstrative of mercy and compassion. A compassionate church is a community of the merciful.

Sacrificing

To serve involves sacrifice. Factually speaking, there is very little serving that does not demand sacrifice on our part. It is costly to serve, which could be the reason why getting members to serve one another inside the church is such a struggle. Doing like Jesus involves living a sacrificial life both in the world and in the church. Our lives are to be *a living sacrifice, holy, acceptable to God which is your spiritual service of worship"* (Romans 12:1, NASB). We discussed the matter of conforming to Jesus earlier in the book; however, now we will address it in the context of sacrifice. The term "sacrifice" is not used much in the church these days. It is a term that is not very pleasant to the ears of self-serving, self-centered saints. However, being like Jesus will lead to sacrifice and suffering (see 2 Corinthians 4:7-12). Like the apostle Paul, Christians are marked out for sacrifice and suffering. In his commentary of 2 Corinthians, Dr. Fred Fisher wrote: *"Those who follow [Jesus] in his glory must follow him also in his cross."*[14] Death was working in the apostle in order that life was manifested in the Corinthians. That was so much like Jesus. Paul sacrificed so the Corinthians could experience life. Sacrifice is what we do voluntarily, and suffering may be involuntary. To sacrifice is to put ourselves at God's disposal. Sacrificing is an act of the will. It is choosing to live on the altar and not merely at the altar. Like Abraham's son Isaac, we voluntarily get upon the altar. Abraham's servants were not around, nor were they needed to put Isaac upon the altar. And even though Isaac was old enough and strong enough to resist and refuse the altar (see Genesis 22), he surrendered to his father's will and voluntarily climbed upon it. Isaac's actions parallel those of Jesus Christ, who would later surrender His will to the will of His Father (see Mark 14:32-42).

As stated above, living in the will of God demands surrender and sacrifice. The sacrificial life, much like the life of a slave, demands that we have no agenda or purpose beyond doing the bidding of the Master. Elisha Hoffman challenges us Christians to live on the altar when he puts lyrics to music:

"Would you walk with the Lord in the light of His word,
and have peace and contentment always?
You must do His sweet will to be free from all ill
on the altar your all you must lay.

"Is your all on the altar of sacrifice laid?
Your heart does the Spirit control?

---

14   Fred Fisher, First & Second Corinthians (Word Books, Waco, Texas, 1975), p. 323.

You can only be blest and have peace and sweet rest
as you yield Him your body and soul."[15]

Altar living must be a way of life if we are to do like Jesus. The dynamic of the Christian life demands being crucified (see Galatians 2:20). Living in the spiritual is attained through sacrificing oneself. The resurrection life was the longing of the apostle Paul (see Philippians 3:10,11), and it ought to be the purpose of the life of every Christian. Resurrection follows crucifixion; you cannot have resurrection without experiencing crucifixion. Becoming like Jesus necessitates conforming to His death. Attaining resurrection is to experience the risen Christ in your life out from among the dead. It is a process of becoming like Jesus through living on the altar. It is the paradox of dying to live (see Philippians 3:7-8). It is losing to win.

Placing ourselves at God's disposal is usually for the benefit of others, but His will is the driving force of the expressions of our sacrificial love for others. This is demonstrated by Paul in 2 Corinthians 4:10-12. He was at the disposal of Christ for the benefit of others, and it was through his sacrificial living that the life of Christ was manifested. Here, being like Jesus resulted in doing like Jesus. We Christians do not desire sacrifice; however, a sacrificial life is a life sanctified for the Master's use, and it is a life that will lead to suffering (Colossians 1:24-29).

Suffering

Because of sin, suffering is common to all humanity, including the cosmos (see Romans 8:18-25). Physical, emotional, mental, relational, social, and natural disasters are all the result of sin. There are self-inflicted sins and social sins that cause suffering (see 1 Peter 4:15). Living in a fallen world produces sufferings of all kind. Suffering is an alien intrusion into God's creation, and all experience it. As stated at the end of the previous

---

15   Elisha A. Hoffman: Hymn: "Is Your All on the Altar."

section, sacrifice leads to suffering, and doing like Jesus requires sacrifice and suffering. The sacrificial life surrenders to the will of God. The sacrificial life is pre-mortem before it is post-mortem—becoming a sacrifice before making a sacrifice. It is a life lived under the will of God; a life that precedes Christian suffering and service. Suffering as a Christian, on the other hand, is different from suffering in the world. Suffering is more personal and pointed for Christians. Christians are the object of suffering for righteousness and Jesus' sake. Paradoxically, Christians ought to be happy in suffering for righteousness and for Jesus' sake (see Matthew 5:10; 1 Peter 3:14-18). The Christian distinctive is found in the reason for suffering. When we suffer because we identify with Christ and His mission in the world, it becomes obvious that we are doing like Him. Congratulatory suffering is involvement in finishing what Christ began to do and teach (see Acts 1:1; Colossians 1:24), taking the blows that were meant for Him. Joy in suffering is not some unhealthy obsession with pain; rather, it is the realization of how God uses it for good (see Romans 5:3-5; 8:28). Through suffering we are drawn closer and deeper in Christ (see Philippians 3:10); it signals that we belong to Christ (see 2 Timothy 3:12; 1 Peter 4:14); it reminds us of future glory (see Romans 8:17-18; 2 Corinthians 4:17); it can influence unbelievers towards salvation (see Philippians 1:12-18); when Christians joyfully suffer for Christ, it frustrates the enemy's plans (see Genesis 50:20-21).

Cross-less Christianity appears to be the order of the day. Christians today desire a painless pilgrimage. They want to reign with Christ without suffering (see 2 Timothy 2:12, KJV). The apostle Paul basically told timid Timothy, "no pain, no gain." Many modern Christians seek a Christianity of convenience that promises "your best life now." The abundant life of Christianity does not speak of the quality of the American life; rather, it speaks of the quality of the new life. Although the Bible speaks of the dangers of riches (see 1 Timothy 6:9-10), being rich is not sinful and poverty is not a characteristic of sainthood. Regardless of whether you have much or little, doing like Jesus will lead to suffering just the same.

The Christian life is evidenced by practicing righteousness (see 1 John 2:29; 3:7-10). Those who are positionally righteous will practice righteousness, and the practice of righteousness will result in suffering (see Matthew 5:10; 1 Peter 3:14-17). God demands righteousness for our reconciliation, and because we have no righteousness of our own that is pleasing to God (see Philippians 3:9), Christ became our righteousness. We are, therefore, benefactors of imputed righteousness (see 2 Corinthians 5:21). On the cross of suffering, Christ took our sins upon Himself in exchange for His righteousness. Imputed righteousness became imparted righteousness in that we through faith in Jesus Christ have received His righteousness and are to, therefore, practice it. We as Christians hunger and thirst for righteousness (see Matthew 5:6), we seek and prioritize it (see Matthew 6:33), we wear it (see Ephesians 6:14), and we practice and suffer for righteousness' sake (see 1 John 3:7; Matthew 5:10). If Christians are not experiencing some form of suffering, perhaps it is because they have conformed to this world instead of being transformed. True believers are not of this world. Heaven-bound people will always clash with the forces of the hell-bound. When Christians seek the principles and the practices of the kingdom of God, the systems of this world will always oppose, oppress, and obstruct the way of the righteous (see Ephesians 6:10-20). Suffering is evidential of to whom you belong. If you be, do, and think like Jesus you will suffer (see John 15:18-22; 2 Timothy 3:12).

One of the strangest truths in Scripture is that God purposes and particularizes suffering for some. By divine setup, God picks you out for suffering according to the providence of God. No sin is involved, no persecution is being experienced, and no dark clouds are gathering over your life. God decides to summon Satan to "bother" you in order that God gets glory. However, God cannot trust everyone with this type of suffering. By way of biblical examples of those whom God did trust with this type of suffering, Job comes to mind. He was recommended by the Lord to experience sufferings at the hand of Satan. *"Then the Lord said to Satan, 'Have you considered My servant Job, that there is none like him on the earth, a blameless and upright man, one who fears God and shuns evil?"'* (Job 1:8, NKJV) The man born blind in the Gospel of John was also divinely set up for the glory of God, thus Jesus said this man's condition was by design (see John 9:3-5). The apostle Paul was given a disability by divine design for a divine purpose (see 2 Corinthians 12:7-10). God allowed Satan to attack him in order for strength to be manifested in human weakness.

As alluded to earlier in this writing, suffering must also be received and understood as a gift (see Philippians 1:29). It is a gift because of what it produces. However, suffering causes us to manifest the life of Christ through our mortal bodies (see 2 Corinthians 4:7-12). When we suffer for Christ's sake we have been graced, for in grace we find our sufficiency in suffering. What a wonderful gift to be a substitute sufferer for Christ. In His absence, we are called to stand in for Him (see Colossians 1:24). Yes! We do like Jesus when we suffer for His name's sake, for righteousness' sake, for the Gospel's sake, and for His glory. Christ suffered for the sake of redemption, and we suffer for righteousness' sake (see Philippians 3:10).

The power of the resurrection is the essence and essentiality of the new life that makes us authentic Christians. This reality makes sharing in the sufferings of Christ inevitable. Conforming to Christ's death is more self-emptying in nature (see Philippians 2:7). It is the willingness to be inconvenienced for the sake of Christ much like He was inconvenienced for the sake of sinners, which was God's purpose for His life. The power of this resurrection is a spiritual reality before it becomes a physical one. Spiritually, we share in Christ's death and resurrection (see Romans 6:1-11). Therefore, the word "resurrection" mentioned in Philippians 3:11 is literally "resurrection out from among" the dead. It could refer to the general physical resurrection (see 1 Corinthians 15) or, as some believe, to the Rapture (see 1 Thessalonians 4:17). However, it is my belief that it refers to a spiritual resurrection resulting in walking in the newness of life (see Romans 6:4), which best fits the context of Philippians 3. Suffering for righteousness' sake distinguishes Christians from those who are spiritually dead. Christians are called to be separate from the world but social in the world. Christians are not of the world (see John 17:14-19) and are not to conform to the world. Nonconformity leads to conflict, and Christianity by nature is not always one with the culture. When a person becomes a Christian, conflict is automatic. This is what Jesus was saying in Matthew 10:34-36. Salvation is evidenced by suffering for the sake of righteousness.

Think It Through

1. *What makes a Christian a Christian?*

2. *Why do you think personhood is more important than performance?*

3. *When is Christianity merely religious?*

4. *When and why is the grace of God frustrated?*

5. *What are the greater works we will do than Christ has done?*

6. *Why is the idea of submission so difficult for us to embrace?*

7. *Explain how spiritual growth is a means of serving one another.*

8. *How did Jesus best serve us?*

9. *What happens when Christians seek to redefine Jesus' ministry and mission?*

10. *Jesus came preaching, teaching, and healing. How is the church to do like Jesus?*

11. *What is the difference between sacrifice and suffering as a Christian?*

CHAPTER

5

Thinking like Jesus

*"We win when each member grows in relationship with Jesus, being, doing, **thinking** like Him, influencing growth and maturity in the body of Christ."*

The ability to think is a wonderful gift from God, and it is a gift that we take for granted until we lose it. You don't want your body to outlive your mind. The mantra of the United Negro College Fund is: "The mind is a terrible thing to waste." This mantra emphasizes the importance of cognitive thinking. Humanity's ability to reason and think is what differentiates human life from insect, plant, and animal life. Humans' God likeness is found in our being rational creatures. Humans are thinkers and are more intelligent than instinctive. The thinking capacity of humans distinguishes them from the ape. It enables people to have self-determination, self-consciousness, and moral consciousness. The human is a cognitive being with volition, and his mind, emotions, and will are at the core of his being. The Psalmist exclaimed, *"For you formed my inward parts; You covered me in my mother's womb. I praise You, for I am fearfully and wonderfully made; marvelous are Your works, and that my soul knows very well"* (Psalm 139:13-14, NKJV). Everything that is seen and unseen originated in the mind of God. God gave humanity dominion over the earth, and everything humanity produces or makes originates in his mind. The mind is a precious and powerful gift and all achievements, advancements, attainments, and accomplishments are conceived in the mind. Rapid advancements in science and technology did not come into existence by fate or by chance, but were once thoughts that were conceived in the mind and then "birthed" into existence. It is very rational for people to accept scientific and technological advances; however, creation is irrational to people. This is asinine. There is nothing more intriguing and intellectually incomprehensible than creation with all its splendor and stupendous properties of creative genius. This gives credence to the fact that there must be a Creator who has a mind.

The capacity to think is evidenced in Adam's ability to distinctively name all the animals in the Garden of Eden. God also gave him the ability to discern prior to his act of disobedience: *"And the Lord God commanded the man, saying, 'of every tree of the garden you may freely eat; of the tree of the knowledge of good and evil you shall not eat, for in the day that you eat of it you shall surely die'"* (Genesis 2:16-17, NKJV). Knowing good and evil was not a bad thing, but ignoring God's command led to death, and that was bad. The motive behind the quest to know good and evil was where the sin was. To seek to be more than you and I were created to be is where sin lies. Thinking beyond or below where God has thought will always lead to sin.

Because of the Fall

Adam and Eve bought Satan's lie and sold the truth for a taste of fruit; herein lies the fall of humanity. Satan led our first parents to question the thinking of God and then revolt against the thinking of God. They went against the One who thought and spoke the world into existence. Satan led an attack on the Word of God. Questioning the reliability of God's Word is not only an ancient strategy, it is a contemporary one. Man, who thinks he has come of age, thinks he can outthink the Thinker by substituting his thinking for God's. This is like an insect attempting to outthink Einstein. Compared to the omniscient God, humanity is like an insect. In the Fall, people did not fall upward, as some suppose; they fell downward. Although they were created by God in the image of God, they were not satisfied with that. They wanted to be more than they were created to be; they wanted divinity. Their pursuit was to become God, even though they were human—a little lower than the angels (see Psalm 8:5). All the advances in science, medicine, technology, social sciences, and psychology make it difficult for some to accept that intelligent humanity fell downward and has been on a downward spiral ever since. Nonetheless, the Bible declares that sin perpetuated death and degeneration. The death proclaimed by the Almighty after the sin of Adam and Eve was a comprehensive death that affected the whole person—body, mind, emotions, will, and relationships. The entire creation is affected by their rebellious deed (see Romans 8:18-25).

The most devastating effect of sin is the corruption of the mind (see Romans 1:28; 2 Corinthians 11:3). In the Fall, the human mind was subtly but seriously impaired. The death pronounced by the Creator upon Adam and Eve was subtle. Although God said that they would surely die, they did not experience death immediately, but gradually (see Genesis 2:17; 3:3, 4). Instead of immediate death, Adam and Eve were expelled from the Garden and experienced tension between each other (Adam and Eve). Because of the subtly of the death sentence, one may think that Satan was correct in contradicting what God had said, that they would surely die. Although death appeared to be elusive, it was inevitable. Moreover, the central core of their being—their mind, their thinking—had been distorted. Listen to the apostle Paul's description:

"For the wrath of God is revealed from heaven against all ungodliness and unrighteousness of men, who suppress the truth in unrighteousness, because what may be known of God is manifest in them, for God has shown it to them. For since the creation of the world His invisible attributes are clearly seen, being understood by the things that are made, even His eternal power and Godhead, so that they are without excuse, because, although they knew God, they did not glorify Him as God, nor were thankful, but became futile in their thoughts, and their foolish hearts were darkened. Professing to be wise, they became fools, and changed the glory of the incorruptible God into an image made like corruptible men—birds and four-footed animals and creeping things. Therefore God also

gave them up to uncleanness, in the lust of their hearts, to dishonor their bodies among themselves, who exchanged the truth of God for the lie, and worshipped and served the creature rather than the Creator, who is blessed forever. Amen" (Romans 8:18-25, NKJV).

This long quote helps us see the downward path of the human mind. Because of sin, humanity's thinking has gone astray (see Isaiah 53:6). The mind is corrupted by sin, and because of sin the truth of God is suppressed. Although intelligent, the human mind is imprudent and impoverished as it relates to godliness. We now live in a world where right is wrong and wrong is right. Truth is relative, and God is seen as only a subjective reality. Many people who are deemed mentally insane possess a high level of intelligence, and there are those with low levels of intelligence who are sane. The wisdom of humanity is basically God-given. God downloaded the mind into the human body and programmed it to think His thoughts, but human rebellion has corrupted human thinking (see 2 Timothy 3:8; Titus 1:15).

The Need for a Renewed Mind

Because of the Fall, humanity desperately needs a renewed and restored mind. Sin has distorted humanity's thinking to the point where he is consumed with his own thoughts rather than the thoughts of God. The god of this world, Satan, desires to keep humankind in the dark (see 2 Corinthians 4:1-6). Basically there are two views of life: the world's view and the Bible's view. Satan blinds people's minds by insisting they have a worldview of life. Education seeks to produce independent thinkers. Parents also desire that their children think for themselves, telling them as they are growing up, *"Don't let anyone think for you; learn to think for yourselves. Whoever thinks for you controls you."* This admonition is difficult to achieve in this social environment. As social creatures, people are influenced by the thinking of the world, driven by political correctness, cultural shifts, and social norms. Although people are individuals with distinct personalities and idiosyncrasies, the world's view shapes their thinking, making it almost impossible for them to think independently, and thus are prisoners of a worldview.

The broadness and diversity of the worldview gives people the illusion of being independent thinkers when, in reality, they are not. People are born conformists. Christians are in the world but not of the world. Christians do not view life and the world from under the sun, but rather above the sun (see Ecclesiastes 2:11). When viewing things from under the sun, the mind is not on things above (see Colossians 3:1-3). These diverse worldviews are found in *nihilism*, which has no sense of existence, *existentialism*, which sees everything as meaningless, *pantheism*, which sees everyone and everything as gods, *atheism*, which claims the non-existence of God, *humanism*, where humanity is self-sufficient, *new age*, where the person is the center point of all reality, *modernism*, where science is the only means of discovering truth, and *post-modernism*, where there is no objective truth and no certainties; all truth is subjective. John MacArthur defines what it means to view life from above the sun (from God's perspective) when he states, *"Truth is that which is consistent with the mind, will, character, glory, and being of God. It is the self-expression of God."*[16] To know truth is to know the mind of God found in the Word of God and personified in the Son of God (see John 1:1, 14; 14:6).

The Mind of Christ

Thinking like Jesus commences in regeneration, continues through sanctification, and is consummated in glorification. Fundamentally, we are able to think like Jesus because in salvation we are given the mind of Christ. In the new birth, we acquire the capacity to understand spiritual truth (see 1 Corinthians 2:14-16). We think like Jesus because repentance has taken place. Repentance deals with the intellect, the emotions, and

---

16   John MacArthur: The Truth War (Nashville, Tennessee, Thomas Nelson, 2007), p.2.

the will. Repentance involves a change or renewal of the mind, a change of the emotions, and a change of the will. There is also a change in attitude towards sin, which causes one to turn from its mastery over our lives. Turning to God is automatically turning from sin (see Acts 2:38; 3:19; 26:18; 1 Thessalonians 1:9). The mind must be restored before it is renewed. As Christians and partakers of the divine nature, a new mind takes up residence in the new person. To be like Jesus is to have the mind of Jesus, which is a present reality that each Christian possesses forever. And certainly having the mind of Christ is having the Spirit of truth (see John 16:12-15). Faith also has to do with the mind, emotions, and will. Faith embraces the truth about God in Christ as true and reliable; with the will, faith surrenders to Christ as Lord; and with heart (the emotions) there is assent to the truth with a keen sense of the need to be saved (see Romans 10:8-21).

In salvation, we are fixed to think God's thoughts. Christianity is not only volitional and emotional; it is intellectual. In many churches, you are not required to bring your mind into the worship experience. In other words, there is no thinking required on Sundays—only feeling. Some congregations do not require that God be worshipped in spirit and truth, but we must not act like mindless creatures. Christianity does require us to think God's thoughts. We must have Christian thinkers. However, these days there is a proliferation of gullible Christians who are not challenged to think biblically but lean on emotions and experience more than the truth of God's Word. In the new birth, we are birthed into the kingdom of God, and His kingdom is by nature a disciplined kingdom. Jesus calls for us to seek the kingdom of God and His righteousness (see Matthew 6:33). This is a call to seek His thinking.

Biblical Thinking

The Bible comes from the mouth and mind of God; it is God-breathed. As He spoke the Word into existence through prophets, apostles, and others,

He penned the literary word about Jesus the Living Word (see 2 Peter 1:20-21). It appears to be narrow to say that only in the Bible we find the thinking of God, but it is true. The worldview of life does not have room for narrowness. One reason is that by nature and intent, the worldview is the broad road—a road that leads to destruction (see Matthew 7:13-14). Biblical thinking is seen as politically incorrect. The exclusivity declared by Jesus Himself is appalling to most people (see John 14:6). Even inside the Christian church, inclusiveness is more appealing. Therefore, to say that God's thinking is limited to the Bible is unthinkable, unintelligible, unreasonable, and unacceptable. In Scripture alone we have the mind of God. But for the omniscient, omnipresent, omnipotent, immense, and transcendent God to have His thinking limited to the sixty-six books of the Bible seems contradictory to His nature. Surely, God who is eternal said more than what is contained in the Bible. Without a doubt, God has said more, but all that He has cared to say to us is confined to the Bible (see John 20:30-31; 21:25). John acknowledged that Jesus did more than what was discovered in His Gospel; however, the Gospel was written to bring people into relationship with God through Jesus Christ. The Bible is about salvation through Jesus Christ alone. The Bible is just a glimpse into the mind of God (see Romans 11:33-36). Essentially, the Bible is God giving us a piece of His mind, but it is the piece of the human puzzle that is most important to the human predicament. The totality of God's mind could not be contained in all the libraries, museums, and depositories in the world. So, why do we have the Bible? Its history, archeology, science, prophecies, unity, and Jesus' use of it says it is as reliable as the mouth and mind of God. The Bible is a "thus says the Lord" book, and both the Old and New Testaments boldly affirm this.

Where else can we find the mind of God (see John 6:68)? Can we trust the *Book of Mormon*, written by one man, Joseph Smith, a plagiarist whose historical and geographical references cannot be validated by independent sources? Can we trust Mohammed's Koran that is also unreliable historically and geographically? Can we trust our experiences of dreams, emotional catharses, visions, new revelations, and private epiphanies? I think not. I would rather trust in the Bible that declares, *"God, who at various times and in various ways spoke in time past to the fathers by the prophets, has in these last days spoken to us by His Son, whom He has appointed heir of all things, through whom also He made the worlds"* (Hebrews 1:1, 2, NKJV).

Biblical Interpretation

Is it possible to discern the mind and thinking of Christ without a sea of varied interpretations of Scripture? Is the Bible open for individual interpretations? How can we think like Jesus when there are so many Christologies? The call to rightly divide the Word of truth (see 2 Timothy 2:15, NKJV) strongly suggests that truth is narrow. Thinking like Jesus cannot be open to private interpretations. For truth to be authentic, it cannot be subjective. Postmodernism thinks truth can be a personal preference. If truth is not objective, it is not truth. Subjective truth has produced many gods, saviors, and religions. Wrongly dividing the Word of truth and other counterfeit writings will lead to untruth. The Bible is the book of objective truth, and the Jesus of the Bible declares that He is the very essence of definitive and objective truth (see John 14:6). The entire Bible is the revelation of Jesus Christ. It would be impossible to think like Jesus apart from the Bible. And furthermore, it would be impossible to think like Jesus if the Bible's authority is suspect. If there is no conviction that the Bible is the revealed, reliable, and relevant Word of God, then how can we discover the thinking of Jesus? We trust in the sufficiency, authority, infallibility, and inerrancy of the sacred Scriptures in order to think like Jesus.

Jesus' thinking is hindered when we only know what the Bible says and not what it means, and to discover the meaning of Jesus' thinking takes work (see 2 Timothy 2:15; 3:10-17). This work is a disciplined journey that demands reading, observation, interpretation, and the application of

Scripture. To discover what the biblical passage meant to the first reader is imperative to arriving at Jesus' thinking in the passage. If we do not understand the historical, grammatical, and literary study of a passage in its context, we will misunderstand Jesus' thinking.

As mentioned above, to understand the thinking of Jesus we must embrace revelation, inspiration, authority, infallibility, and inerrancy, but we must not forget illumination. We know the Holy Spirit is essential to inspiration (see 2 Peter 1:20, 21), but we know little of His work in illumination (see 1 Corinthians 2:9-16). We cannot think like Jesus without the illumination of the Spirit. Information is attained by reading, studying, and researching books in your library, but only through the Holy Spirit do you have illumination. The illumination of the Spirit makes alive the Word of God, enabling you to understand the meaning of the Word in a personal way. Illumination is the means by which God makes His Word personal to you; it is not some new revelation of truth. Through illumination you will see the revealed truth which transforms your thinking and behavior (see Psalm 119:18).

Illumination is like the Spirit walking down your street and lifting the scales from your eyes. It is like a light coming on in your heart and mind and your response is, "I got it." The Holy Spirit is the indwelling Teacher who illuminates the mind to comprehend the Word (see John 14:25-26). It is often said that the anointing of God is on your life, but the reality is that the anointing is not on you but in you. Every believer is anointed with the indwelling presence of the Holy Spirit (see 1 John 2:20-27; 3:24–4:4). The anointing is a one-time experience that happens in the past with the abiding presence of the Holy Spirit who protects believers from false teachers and false teaching. The oil of anointing is the symbolic presence of the Holy Spirit in the believer. Without the continuous inner work of the Holy Spirit, believers would not be able to think like Jesus. The absence of Christian influence in the world can be attributed to Christians' not thinking like Jesus. It is said that most Christians who claim to be born again do not possess a biblical worldview. These Christians bear the name and, hopefully, the nature, but they are not being transformed by the renewing of their minds. Simply having the mind of Christ is not enough. Christians must develop the mind of Christ within themselves. Christians who do not think like Jesus are thinking like the world, conforming to the world's mindset (see Romans 12:1, 2). The thinking and behavior of Christians are worldly if they are not experiencing transformation by the renewing of the minds.

The Holy Spirit, who is our inner intercessor and instructor, collaborates with the will and Word of God and guides us into all truth, assisting us in telling the truth about Jesus, who is the Truth (see John 16:5-15; Acts 1:8). As intercessor, the Holy Spirit is also our prayer partner (see Romans 8:26-27). He knows the mind of our Father God, and the Father knows the mind of the Spirit, for the Holy Spirit, the Father, and Jesus Christ the Son are one. The Holy Trinity is at work within us to assist us to think righteously like Jesus, which enables us to live righteous lives. Proverbs 23:7 says, *"For as [a man] thinks in his heart, so is he."* The thought life can determine behavior, whether good or bad, which is why we find these words in Scripture: *"Finally, brethren, whatever things are true, whatever things are noble, whatever things are just, whatever things are pure, whatever things are lovely, whatever things are of good report, if there is any virtue and if there is anything praiseworthy—meditate on these things"* (Philippians 4:8).

To think like Jesus requires that we rightly identify ourselves as saints and not sinners. Possessing the mentality of a saint leads to saintlike actions. Possessing the mentality of a sinner leads to sinner-like actions. Identifying with the first Adam is unhealthy. We must identify with the Second Adam and think like Christ. We were sinners but now we are saints because we have been delivered from the power of sin, not the presence of sin (see Romans 6:1-14). Our position and practice as believers is righteousness.

We have imputed and imparted righteousness (see Romans 4:22-25; 1 John 2:29; 3:7, 10). As Christians we hunger and thirst to become who we already are in Christ Jesus—righteous (see Matthew 5:6; 6:33). When we think correctly about who we are in Christ Jesus, we will behave in a godly manner (see 1 John 3:3). Wrongly interpreting the doctrine of grace and the security of the believer can lead to ungodly behavior, which is an indicator of wrong thinking or, at worse, an unregenerate heart. Remember, thinking like Jesus is preceded by being like Jesus and doing like Jesus.

Battle for the Mind

There is a struggle in the mind and for the mind of Christians. If we can win the battle for the mind and in the mind we will experience God's victory. The will of God will be done in your life, and His purpose in life and in ministry will be realized if the battle is won in the mind and for the mind. The Christian's enemies—the devil, the flesh, and the world's system—are after our minds. They are waging war against the mind in order to keep you and me from thinking like Jesus. The enemies of Christ and His church do not want Christians to behave like Jesus, nor do they want the church to be the church of Jesus Christ. The devil knows how important the mind is and thus seeks to corrupt it. The devil knows that Scripture is the mind of God and, therefore, if he can discredit the Bible by declaring it to be unreliable and irrelevant, he can alter or change Christians' minds with regard to thinking like Jesus. If the devil can make Christians disinterested in growing in grace and in the knowledge of Jesus Christ, then thinking like Jesus will not be their quest. As Christians, we are to put on the whole armor of God. Although the spiritual armor comes in salvation, we must not rely on our past experience. Putting on the armor calls for us to be aggressive participants, not passive (see Ephesians 6:10-18). One of the functions of the armor has to do with protecting the mind: the belt of truth protects the emotions, the breastplate of righteousness protects the heart, the Gospel of peace protects the feet, the shield of faith protects the whole body, the helmet of salvation protects the head, and the sword of the Spirit protects from a frontal attack. Finally, prayer protects us from self-reliance. Putting on the whole armor is a reminder that the Old Ship of Zion is not a luxury liner, but a battleship.

Jesus' temptation experience, waged as an attack on physical weakness, was also a mind battle with Satan (see Matthew 4:1-11). Jesus responded to the temptation by rightly dividing the Word of God. Jesus answered the satanic attack with God's thinking (see Deuteronomy 8:3; Psalm 91:11; Deuteronomy 6:13-14). Jesus did what our first parents failed to do, and that is to answer Satan with the rightly divided Word of God (see Genesis 3:1-6). Satan always attacks the mind first and foremost.

"For the weapons of our warfare are not carnal but mighty in God for pulling down strongholds, casting down arguments and every high thing that exalts itself against the knowledge of God, bringing every thought into captivity to the obedience of Christ, and being ready to punish all disobedience when your obedience is fulfilled" (2 Corinthians 10:4-6, NKJV).

In the battle for the mind, we wage war against false teachings.

Satanic forces and the worldly system present a challenge for Christians to think like Jesus. The devil is the father of lies and stands against truth and fights against truth in unseemly respectful ways. He is the father of lies and uses human wisdom and reasoning to thwart truth and righteousness. He uses human logic and liberties to attempt to undermine righteousness. Human rights now stand against divine righteousness. The prophet Isaiah critiqued these modern times when he said, *"Justice is turned back, and righteousness stands afar off; for truth is fallen in the street, and equity cannot enter. So truth fails, and he who departs from evil makes himself a prey"* (Isaiah 59:14-15, NKJV).

Modernism that focused on rationalism was once Satan's strategy, but then modernism bowed to postmodernism and human subjectivity which states that everyone does what is right according to the individual. I am afraid that Western democracy is headed towards relativism, where truth is uncertain. Such freedom allows persons to determine what is right and wrong for them. Objective truth is viewed as arrogance. Satan's subtle weapons for combating the mind are rationalism, relativism, and human rights. *"There is a way that seems right to a man, but its end is the way of death"* (Proverbs 14:12, NKJV). Truth by divine design is narrow, which bothers post-modern society, which is broad in its thinking (see Matthew 7:13-14). As Christians, our truth is narrow because it is found in God's mind and His Word. Our truth is ontological before it is epistemological, which means that it is not about *what* is truth (see John 18:38), rather it is about *who* is truth (see John 14:6). Truth is narrow because God's Son is the center of veracity, and the Bible is the revelation of Him.

In addition to the two views (world view and Bible view, as mentioned earlier in this book), there are two basic mindsets: the biblical mindset and the non-biblical mindset. People do not function independently of either of these mindsets and, in fact, we are consciously or unconsciously influenced by one or the other. Our life lenses are shaped by various influences: people, teachers, friends, enemies, coworkers, spouses, children, entertainers, sports figures, politicians, public opinions, new media, circumstances, disappointments, history, science, religion, philosophies, and so forth. The impact of the non-biblical mindset is tremendous. Thinking otherworldly is a great challenge living in this world (see Ephesians 6:11-12). When Satan is in the equation, the influential spirit of the age makes thinking like Jesus a miracle (see Ephesians 2:1-10). We must not forget the flesh (see Galatians 5:16, 17). The three enemies that hinder Christians from thinking like Jesus are the devil, the flesh (see Romans 8:7, 8), and the world's system (see 1 Corinthians 3:18-23). The battle for the mind began with Satan's attack on the minds of Adam and Eve. It affected the thinking of the entire human race. The seed of doubt placed in their minds made them question God's care and concern for them. Satan attacked the Word of God at that time, and he is still attacking the Word of God today. Men are still declaring that the Bible cannot be trusted because they believe that the Bible was authored by fallible men. It is therefore their belief that the Bible is unreliable. The Bible contains the thoughts of Jesus; therefore, how then can we trust that which comes from an unreliable source? Nature speaks, but not with clarity. Noncanonical books speak, but not with reliability. Ancient philosophers speak, but not with divine authority. Therefore, the answer is simple. There is no way we can know His thoughts apart from the Bible, the Word of God. Thinking like Jesus is thinking biblically. God has spoken (see Matthew 4:4) in and through His Son (see Mark 9:7). The only definitive word from God is in and through His Son (see Hebrews 1:1, 2). God has spoken sufficiently in and through His Son as stated is sacred Scripture. If the Bible is obliterated, then all we will have for guidance is a sphere of subjective truth. Without the Bible, there is no standard of righteousness and no definitive path to the true and living God. It is the desire of Satan to rid the world of the Bible because it alone tells of the need and provision for human redemption. Since there is no redemptive provision for fallen angels, Satan wishes to blind humanity to their possibility of redemption (see 2 Corinthian 4:3-4).

Erroneous thinking about the Father, the Son, and the Holy Spirit has eternal consequences. If we are to think like Jesus, the mind must be protected because we are involved in a spiritual warfare that is aimed at debilitating the mind of Christ in us. Being involved in this type of battle requires spiritual armor on us and the Spirit of Truth at work within us. Human strength and wisdom are useless for this type of warfare. There are demonic fortresses (ideologies) in the mind that are determined to confront biblical truths (God's thoughts), keep sinners in darkness, and hinder Christians from conforming to the likeness of Christ (see Colossians 1:13). If we are to think like Jesus we must know the Bible, not books about the Bible. Thinking biblically means bleeding and sweating the Bible, which is an essential part of our DNA, and we know that we cannot live by bread alone but by every word that comes from the mouth of God (see Deuteronomy 8:3). When we think like Jesus, we quote the Bible more than commentaries and other books, and since the Word of God is dwelling richly in us, our response to life and the situations and challenges of life is, *"It is written"* (see Matthew 4:1-11).

Those who think like Jesus delight *"in the Law of the Lord; and in his Law they mediate day and night. And they shall be like trees planted by the rivers of water, that brings forth fruit in their season; their leaves also shall not wither; and whatsoever they do shall prosper"* (Psalm 1:2-3).

Those who think like Jesus proclaim, *"Your word is a lamp to my feet, and a light to my path"* (Psalm 119:105).

Those who think like Jesus declare, *"Your word I have hidden in my heart, that I might not sin against You"* (Psalm 119:11).

Those who think like Jesus exclaim *"let this mind be in you, which was also in Christ Jesus; who being in the form of God, thought it not robbery to be equal with God; but made himself of no reputation, and took upon him the form of a servant, and was made in the likeness of men: and being found in fashion as a man, he humbled himself, and became obedient unto death, even the death of the cross"* (Philippians 2:5-9).

Thinking like Jesus is to know the truth that sets you free to be like Jesus, to do like Jesus, and to think like Jesus (see John 8:31, 32). It is a battle for truth against the untruths that keep sinners from Christ and Christians from thinking like Him. When the worldview captures the thinking processes, coming to Christ and growing in grace and knowledge of Christ are impossible. The false teachers in the Corinthian church were impeding evangelism and discipleship, so the apostle Paul saw himself in a battle against their false doctrine (see 2 Corinthians 10:3-5). The sword of the Spirit, which is the Word of God, is necessary to change how we think (see Ephesians 6:17).

Benefits

Spiritual discernment is one of the benefits of thinking like Jesus. In a world where we are faced with a plethora of decisions, spiritual discernment is important. Making wrong decisions with regard to our friends, mates, careers, and the like lead to many painful circumstances. (Making a decision to give one's life to Christ was purposely and theologically omitted from these examples because in this case, the decision is not solely based on people. As in creation, God is the prime mover in salvation and, by faith, the sinner surrenders to the wooing and convicting power of the Holy Spirit. Faith is less about what we do and more about recognizing there is nothing we can do but trust in the Christ of Calvary.)

Thinking like Jesus is invaluable to making decisions. Thinking like Jesus leads to glorifying and pleasing God (see John 8:29). The Spirit of truth through the Word of truth guides the believer to walk in truth, and live out what is true of Jesus.

The problem with some Christians is they do not acknowledge the Lord in all their ways in order for Him to direct their paths (see Proverbs 3:5, 6). God is ready through the illuminating work of the Spirit to shine light on the revealed Word to give us spiritual discernment for life's journey. An apologist is a defender of the faith. Every believer is called to be an apologist (see Jude 3, 4). Thinking like Jesus enables the believer to contend for the faith. Rather than make excuses, we are to give an exegetical explanation for the reason of our hope (see 1 Peter 3:15). When we think biblically like Jesus, we are able to logically and systematically convey why we are Christians. When our life as a Christian exegetes the truth, it will afford us the opportunity to give a verbal reason for our hope. Again, this is why being like Jesus and doing like Him precedes thinking like Him. The exegetical life of the believer is just as important—if not more important—as the exegetical proclamation. To contend for the faith is to fight for the entire body of truth concerning our salvation found in Scripture (see Galatians 1:23; Ephesians 4:13; Philippians 1:27). To contend for the faith will enable stability in the faith (see Ephesians 4:14) while living in a heterodidactic age (see Galatians 1:6-10). In this age of different gospels and aberrant teachings, we must rediscover the thinking of Jesus through rightly dividing the Word of Truth.

Jesus Himself is the personification of wisdom (see 1 Corinthians 1:20-25), and when we think like Jesus we experience the wisdom of God, and we embrace His wisdom in redemption. It is not philosophical wisdom but God's wisdom that accomplishes human salvation, and although it was considered by the Greeks to be foolishness and by the Jews to be a stumbling block, it had redemptive power. Intellectualism is exercising the mind through reasoning, knowing, and thinking to the degree where emotions are excluded. However, to think the thoughts of God is to think beyond the mundane (see Isaiah 55:6-9). Divine wisdom is thinking like Jesus, who is the Wisdom of God. This will put you at odds with the world (see 1 Corinthians 1:18-25). To be a witness in the world, Christians are to be different fundamentally and in our thinking. As Christians, we cannot make a difference until we are different. We are so much like God when we set our minds on things above (see Colossians 3:2). Righteous thinking will break friendship with the world (see James 4:4). However, as Christians we must not fear being countercultural. We must know that our pursuit of the mind of Christ will lead to political incorrectness, as well as persecution upon ourselves and the church. Although we live in a democratic society and a land of religious freedom, we had better be ready for a time of trials and testing as we become the object of scorn and persecution. It will also be a time of sifting to determine who the Christians are in name only and who are Christians in nature.

Churches and Christians who are friends with the world will be invited to the affairs of state. They will become the counselors of kings, prime ministers, and presidents because they will tell the world what they want to hear. There will be no seat at the world's tables of power for Elijah, Elisha, Jeremiah, Amos, Micaiah, and other prophets who will speak truth to power (see 1 Kings 22). There are those who only speak truth to power concerning social issues, and then there are others who will speak truth to power concerning sin which is the cause of social and spiritual problems. It is the Jesus of Calvary, not Capernaum, that will place the church and Christians in opposition to the world. It is the Christ of Calvary that caused the Jews to stumble and the Greeks to declare the message and mission of Jesus as foolish, who will also scorn the church. Jesus the sin bearer and not the social liberator was the subject of scorn. They never would have crucified Him if He would have fulfilled what they perceived was His messianic role. At Calvary, Jesus declared the world sinful, worthy of death, but unable to pay the price and live; and it was there at Calvary where He paid what humanity owed (see 2 Corinthians 5:21). As He thought the universe into existence, so He thought salvation into human history. My friends, this is the wisdom of God (see 1 Corinthians 1:26-31). Wisdom comes from God (see James 1:5). God grants wisdom to those who discipline themselves to think like Jesus. Duplicity in your thinking will not gain you wisdom from God, and there can be no duplicity in thinking like Jesus. Wisdom is the divine ability to handle life with skill and grace. Knowledge without wisdom will lead to the misuse of knowledge. James Merritt makes an insightful observation, when he said, *"We are living in a world that is drowning in knowledge, yet starving for wisdom."*[17] Wisdom helps us come to terms that we know very little. Those who think they have reached the pinnacle of knowledge in any or all subjects lack wisdom. Thinking like Jesus is not having superior knowledge, which the Gnostics claimed, but possessing the mind of Christ in humility (see Philippians 2:5).

---

17   James Merritt: Friends, Foes & Fools (Broadman & Holman Publishers, Nashville, Tennessee, 1997), p. 27.

His Thoughts Are Antithetical

Our thoughts must integrate with the thoughts of Jesus. His thought patterns were incompatible with the thinking of the world around Him. Even His disciples struggled with His thoughts (see Matthew 13:36; Mark 8:31-33). His thoughts about death were incompatible with His disciples' thoughts. If His disciples were baffled, certainly the world was baffled by His perceived oddness. In an upside-down world, uprightness looks odd. Through the incarnation, Jesus became like us in order that we would become like Him. He became like us but more than us (see Philippians 2:7). He is fully man but much more than man, not in reference to His divinity but His humanity. The oddness of Jesus' humanity is His sinlessness (see 2 Corinthians 5:21; Hebrews 4:15; 1 Peter 2:22; 1 John 3:5). He is incompatible with fallen humanity, but invaluable to human recovery (see 2 Corinthians 5:17-21). Jesus identifies with humanity becoming relevant, yet in life and thought He is incompatible. In His mind, enemies are to be loved (see Matthew 5:43-44). In His mind, heavenly treasure are more valuable than earthly gain (see Matthew 6:19-21). In the mind of Jesus, losing is winning (see Matthew 10:39; 16:24-27). In the mind of Jesus, greatness was found in humility and service (see Matthew 18:1-5; 20:25-28; 23:11-12). Jesus taught in antithetical (or opposing) terms when He said you are to be happy when you are poor, persecuted, sad, weak, hungry and thirsty, merciful, and peacemakers (see Matthew 5:1-12). His beatitudes ought to be our attitudes as members of the kingdom of heaven. The way we think separates us from the fandom crowd, making us obedient followers of Christ. Thinking, doing, and being like Jesus will determine our Christology.

Think It Through

1. What is the correlation between the existence of the universe and the mind?

2. What happened to the human mind after the fall of Adam and Eve?

3. Why does the human mind need renewal?

4. What does it mean to have the mind of Christ?

5. What is necessary to think biblically?

6. Why must there be biblical interpretation to know the mind of Christ?

7. Why must the battle be won in the mind?

8. What are the benefits of thinking biblically?

9. In what sense was Jesus' thinking antithetical to the thinking of this age?

CHAPTER

Influencing Growth in the Body of Christ

*"We win when each member grows in relationship with Jesus, being, doing, thinking like Him, **influencing growth** and maturity in the body of Christ."*

When we grow in relationship with Jesus—being, doing, thinking like Him—we become influential witnesses in the world. The mission of the church is to influence the world for Christ. Sharing the Gospel is vital to the evangelization of the world as the body of Christ expands as Christians share their experience of the power of the Gospel. The Gospel must be shared verbally and visibly. Christians must first *be* Good News to really be effective in spreading the Gospel. It is true that sinners must hear the Gospel in order to be saved (see Romans 10:13, 14), but the results of hearing the Gospel are more effective if they can see the Gospel. Because hearing the Gospel suggests the need for a herald, the preacher is essential to the hearing of the Gospel. While I am fully aware of the specificity of the call to preach (see Jeremiah 1:5; Galatians 1:15, 16), reaching the world with the Gospel will not happen if there is no general call to preach (see Acts 8:4). Sanctuary preaching by licensed and ordained men or women will not accomplish Jesus' global vision, arming those in the pew to take the gospel to the streets will. While we debate on who is authorized to preach in pulpits, there is little concern for commissioning saints to take the Gospel to where lost people live, work, play, and learn.

The Pragmatic Strategy for Evangelism

Methods of evangelism are forever evolving. We are constantly seeking new strategies for reaching the lost with the Gospel. Some strategies that have been used in attempts to reach sinners for Christ are the "bus and the block" ministries, canvassing, revivals/crusades, social ministries, seeker sensitive worships, and multimedia. We love to say that the message must remain the same but the methods must change to reach this present age, but could the need to change be due to the fact that we have given up on the Great Commission method in reaching the world for Christ? Jesus mandated believers to have a mobile strategy for reaching the world with the Gospel. While they were going about their regular affairs, they were to make disciples. They were not necessarily called to go out of their way; rather, wherever they were they were to make disciples. Wherever they lived, worked, learned, and played, they were to understand they were on mission. In their concentric circles of influence, believers are to do more than invite people to their gatherings. They are to be inviting through their behavior, generating questions about the hope that is within them.

Lazarus was dead and in the grave for four days before Jesus raised him from the dead (see John 11:1-44). Many unbelievers became believers when they saw a miracle walking among them (see John 12:9-11). Lazarus did not have to speak a word and yet he had tremendous influence on the people with whom he came in contact. He was simply being a witness (see Acts 1:8). When Jesus informed His disciples of their relationship to the world, He was primarily letting them know that they were to be influential in the world (see Matthew 5:13-16). Influence is not gained verbally, influence is gained visually. Jesus said that His disciples would be fishers of men (see Matthew 4:19). To catch fish, one must have attractive bait as well as mended and clean nets (see Matthew 4:21; Luke 5:2).

The Provocative Question

What would I have if I had Jesus? This is the question that is on the minds of much of humanity who find themselves trapped on the raggedy edge of life, marooned in meaninglessness and hopelessness. It is an honest question to ask those who claim to know Jesus personally, and who better to pose this question to than those who have experienced Him? The people who are asking this question are not seeking a deep theological response, or even a biblical response to their question. They do not desire a sermon or a speech. What they do want is a pragmatic response to their provocative question. They would like the response to be experiential and demonstrative. They desire a visible sighting of a genuine Christian, not a pontificator. Those who are enquiring want to see the personification of the Gospel. In this hopeless world, helpless man wants to see the embodiment of hope (see 1 Peter 3:15-17).

What difference would it make in my life if I had Jesus? Is anyone in your concentric circle of influence questioning you concerning the hope that is within you? Are they getting a taste of the spiritual fruit that is being produced in your life (see Galatians 5:22, 23)? Are they sensing that the Lord is good and desiring to place their trust in Him (see Psalm 34:8)? As you grow in relationship with Jesus—being, doing, and thinking like Him—the godly character of the fruit of the Spirit will become more obvious in you.

Transforming Power

The transforming power of the Holy Spirit is evidential in the life of a believer and produces a Christian whose life is influential and abundant. The Holy Spirit's power delivers the sinner from death to life (see John 5:24), from darkness to light (see 1 Peter 2:9), from condemnation to justification (see Romans 8:1-4), from the old to the new (see Romans 6:4), from sinner to saint (see Romans 6:22), and from unrighteousness to righteousness (see 1 John 3:4-10). That is a radical, transformative change which has occurred in the life of the new believer from the inside out due to the indwelling presence of the Holy Spirit! The Christian influence is enabled by the permanent presence of the Holy Spirit (see Luke 24:49; Acts 1:8; Ephesians 5:18). The Greater One within the believer makes positive Christian influence possible. I specify "positive" influence because it is possible for Christians to have a negative influence which nullifies the Christian witness (see Matthew 5:13-16). Positive Christian influence comes from the same power that raised Jesus from the grave (see Romans 8:4), and it is the only influence that makes a difference in this dark world. The Christian life is about transforming, not conforming. Christians are to be transformed by the renewing of the mind. Christians can only make a difference by being different.

Genuine Christians who are being transformed make up the church (the *ecclesia*) of Jesus Christ and are called out from darkness, transformed, and then sent back into darkness to be light (see 1 Thessalonians 5:4-8; 1 Peter 2:9). We cannot be worldly and expect to evangelize the world with the Gospel. Going back to Lazarus' story depicted earlier in this chapter, there is no record in Scripture that Lazarus uttered a single word and yet he caused many to believe on the Lord Jesus Christ. This is because Lazarus was a living miracle, an example of the power of Jesus in a person's life. His life was so convincing that the enemies of Jesus put a hit out on both him and Jesus. His witness was so credible that he would have been a candidate for the witness protection program. What a testimony!

Who are you influencing for Christ? Do your unsaved friends, co-workers, and relatives have more influence over your life than you have over theirs? Is your influence strong enough that at least they respect you as a Christian? Is it obvious to them that you love Jesus? Obnoxious Christianity will turn them off quickly, and they will not respect you as a Christian but view your love for Christ as plastic (see 1 Peter 2:11, 12).

To have influence, you must learn the difference between being in the world and being of the world (see John 17:14-19). Thinking like Jesus is so important because it helps to guard you from being of the world, and in order to think like Jesus, we must know the Word. Conforming to the world is becoming more prevalent among the saints because of biblical illiteracy. You cannot think like Jesus outside of knowing the Bible.

Eternal life is the life of tomorrow given in the now (see John 10:28). Eternal life is time measured by infinity, and a type of life measured by divinity. What is meant by infinity is everlasting life with Jesus, and what is meant by divinity is we are partakers of the divine nature expressed in the fruit of the Spirit. In a sense, eternal life is both quantitative and qualitative. It is both time and type. Eternal life makes us more than earthlings; we are otherworldly. In a spiritual sense, we are "ETs" (extraterrestrials) who are looking to go home (see Hebrews 11:13-16; 1 Peter 2:11, 12). We are ambassadors for Christ. We live and represent the King in a foreign land (see 2 Corinthians 5:20; Ephesians 6:20).

New Growth

The Church must seek new growth and not merely transfer growth, which is not real growth. Transfer growth is when Christians simply change church memberships. Angels in heaven do not rejoice over transfer growth (see Luke 15:10).

We influence new growth in the body of Christ as we pursue the win. Members growing in relationship with Jesus, being, doing, and thinking like Him, will facilitate growth from the inside out. Growth through multiplication is healthy growth. When mature Christians have spiritual children and are involved in nurturing them, the church grows healthier (see Galatians 4:19; 1 Thessalonians 2:7). Mature disciples make disciples. New growth in the body best takes place when we make, mark, mature, and multiply disciples. When we make disciples who are obedient followers of Christ and incorporate them into the fellowship of the church and help them grow in relationship with Jesus and other believers, the result is a healthy church.

Relational Evangelism

Influential growth presupposes establishing relationships with the unsaved, which is relational evangelism as opposed to non-relational evangelism. Non-relational evangelism is spontaneous evangelism which involves evangelizing a person with whom no personal relationship has been developed. This type of evangelism happens when you go to witness instead of witnessing as you go.

Participating in an evangelism outing for the day is event evangelism and is non-relational. This type of evangelism is not about forming relationships, but winning souls. The sinner is asked questions with the hope of leading him or her to make a decision for Christ. If the questions are mostly answered in the affirmative, the person is declared saved. The sinner has engaged in a cognitive experience and, hopefully, a conversion experience. The plan of salvation has been executed, but has the sinner encountered Christ? Spontaneous (or non-relational) evangelism has its moments. It may be your only opportunity to share the Gospel with a person, which will often be the case when sitting next to a fellow traveler on a plane, bus, or train and there is no time to cultivate a relationship, but the opportunity to share the Gospel has presented itself. Whenever we are afforded the opportunity to sow the Gospel, we are to sow the Gospel.

Relational evangelism is best suited for the sinner to encounter Christ in a personal way. In this approach to evangelism the witness, while sanctifying the Lord in his or her heart, is asked about the hope that is within them (see 1 Peter 3:15). In relational evangelism, the witness shares Christ in the light of sharing the new life. The "as you go" method of relational evangelism is purposeful and intentional. Relational evangelism involves the believer's preparing the way for the unbelieving friend, neighbor, coworker, and/ or relative to respond to the Gospel through their relationship with the believer and the believer's relationship with Jesus. This type of evangelism brings to mind the ministry of John the Baptist as he prepared the way of the Lord (see Matthew 3:3). I don't mean to make light of any opportunity to share the Gospel, because the urgency and the uncertainty of the times calls for all forms of evangelism (relational, non-relational, and visible) to be implemented.

The Fruit of the Spirit

Let me now return to the provocative question: *What would I have if I had Jesus?*

Influencing growth in the body of Christ is greatly enhanced when saints can pragmatically respond to this question. Let me suggest that the manifestation of the fruit of the Spirit in the life of the believer is a positive response. The fruit of the Spirit is worked in and worked out by the Spirit. We do not produce the fruit nor do we perform them on our own. The fruit belongs to the Spirit, is produced by the Spirit, and is executed in us by the power of the Spirit. The nine graces found in Galatians 5:22 are a matter of God's grace. The life of the Holy Spirit in us as we yield to Him allows the manifestation of the fruit planted in us at regeneration. The influence of the visible witness will give substance to the verbal witness. Elton Trueblood said:

"The spoken word is never really effective unless it is backed up by a life, but it is also true that the living deed is never adequate without the support which the spoken word can provide. This is because no life is ever good enough. The person who says naively, 'I don't need to preach; I just let my life speak,' is insufferably self-righteous. What one among us is so good that he can let his life speak and leave it at that?"[18]

---

18 Elton Trueblood: The Company of the Committed (Harper & Row Publishers, New York, 1961), p. 53.

The fruit of the Spirit is in the singular although it comes to believers in bunches at regeneration. The fruit describes Christian character that derives from being like Jesus. As God is love, the Christian who possesses the nature of God demonstrates and displays *love* vertically towards God and horizontally towards people (see 2 Peter 1:4; 1 John 4:7-11). Years ago, recording artist Dionne Warwick sang a song that contained the following lyrics: *"What the world needs now is love, sweet love."* Love is a beautiful human expression, but if it is not upward towards God and outward from God, it is out of bounds and out of control. The moral attitude of this age is captured in the words of another song: *"If loving you is wrong, I don't want to be right."* We are to worship God, who is love, rather than love. Essentially, love is only right when it is contextualized in righteousness which is God's standard of right. All human expressions of love must start with the greatest commandment: *"Hear, O Israel: The Lord our God, the Lord is One! You shall love the Lord your God with all your heart, with all your soul, and with all our strength"* (Deuteronomy 6:4, 5; see also, Matthew 22:37-40). Furthermore, all expressions of love must be governed by what Jesus exclaimed: *"If you love Me, keep My commandments"* (see John 14:15, 23, 24). You should not expect Jesus to accept your demonstrations of love when it is an anti-God expression. Living to please God is what shapes Christian character (see 1 Thessalonians 4:1-5). Having Jesus is having the love of God in your heart (see Romans 5:5). This is the same love that Jesus had for you, which is an unconditional, sacrificial love. Your love for others should be driven by Christ's love for you (see John 13:34, 35). As the beloved of God, we are able to love others as Christ loved us (see 1 John 3:1-3). Only those who have experienced the redemptive love of Christ can properly love others. Therefore, love is sacrificing to achieve God's best for another person. Christ-like virtues and deeds that flow from our redemptive experience of love make us Christians contagious and attractive. This is what influences growth in the body of Christ.

What would I have if I had Jesus? One response of Christians to this provocative question is *joy*. The disposition of joy is the strength of the Christian influence in this world. Joy and happiness are not synonymous. Happiness is contingent upon occurrences, but joy celebrates an inward confidence and contentment that is from the Lord. What makes believers' joy so amazing is that it shines best in darkness. In the midst of hopelessness Nehemiah declared, *"Do not sorrow, for the joy of the Lord is your strength"* (Nehemiah 8:10). The believer's joy is influential because it gives us songs in the night in a strange land (see Psalm 137:1-6). The believer's joy is an enabling joy (see 1 Thessalonians 1:6; Romans 14:17). This God-given joy operates best in a strange land. The strength of joy is that it operates in weakness (see 2 Corinthians 12:10). It is uncharacteristic of Christians to be consumed with sadness. As children of the day, we usher in joy in the morning (see 1 Thessalonians 5:5; Psalm 30:5). The joy that the Holy Spirit produces in us comes from hope. We live and die in hope. Hope is the certainty of a reality not yet experienced (see Romans 5:1-5; 15:13). The Believer's joy is nurtured through the providential will of God (see Romans 8:28). The fruit of the Spirit, unlike the gifts of the Spirit, is to be displayed in the world. Christian joy is an instrument of evangelism. The gifts of the Spirit are designed to equip believers, while the fruit of the Spirit is designed to reach unbelievers. Through the fruit of the Spirit heaven comes down to earth. Speaking about Christians, Jerry Vines quotes Nietzsche, the atheist: *"You are going to have to look more redeemed than you do if we are to believe the message of redemption."*[19] Dr. Vines further says, *"If we are full of the Holy Spirit we should radiate the fullness of joy to those we meet."*[20]

What would I have if I had Jesus? Another response of Christians would be *peace*. People are in search of peace, but there is no real peace in this world. They may search but cannot find it; they cannot negotiate it,

---

19 Jerry Vines: Spirit Fruit (Broadman & Holman Publishers, Nashville, Tennessee, 2001), p. 50.

20 Ibid., p. 50.

militarize it, or gain it through sanctions. Peace treaties are temporary at best, and there is no one who can legitimately qualify for the Nobel Peace prize. The ultimate qualifier for peace is Jesus, who is the Prince of Peace (see Isaiah 9:6). Real peace comes only from God through Jesus. Peace came to earth through the incarnation. Peace was on earth because He who was designated to make peace through the blood of the everlasting covenant was here (see Hebrews 13:20, 21). It may seem strange, but Jesus came to earth to divide and through His death, unite (see Luke 12:49-53; Ephesians 2:14-18). There can be no peace with one another until there is first peace with God. The human plight is their enmity with God. God and humanity are in a state of war. This is the tragic condition of separation, and it must be remedied before there can be peace. Human sin separated God and humanity (see Isaiah 59:2). It is this problem that prevents any kind of peace on earth. A world in rebellion against God will never experience peace on earth.

Jesus came not to offer superficial peace, but deal with the root of humanity's restlessness. Christ came into the world to bring calm to the storm within people. He came not simply to deal with the symptoms, but the cause. The need for peace with God is at the very core of the human plight, plunge, and predicament. Reconciliation is necessary if peace is to be experienced, and this can only happen in and through Christ of Calvary (see 2 Corinthians 5:17-21; Ephesians 2:14, 15; Colossians 1:20). The characteristic of peace that identifies believers as Christians is the result of having peace with God (see Romans 5:1, 2). We have experienced peace with God; therefore, we are able to express it and be an influence in the world. Now we have the peace that belongs to God that defies understanding. It is incomprehensible peace that influences the world for Christ (see Philippians 4:7). It is a peace that shows up in the midst of the storms of life (see Mark 4:35-41). As Christians grow in relationship with Jesus, they will discover peace in His presence. Jesus promised His disciples and every believer that they would have peace (see John 14:27; 16:33). This peace is exclusively the property of believers. The peace of God shows up at strange times, circumstances, and situations. When the world sees this peace that is in us, it wants what we have. It is such a calming peace that the world thinks we are on some performance-enhancing substance. Yes! This peace is enabled by the performance-enhancing Spirit. When this peace is operative in the life of the believer, it pragmatically answers the query, *"What would I have if I had Jesus?"* It is peace from another country—peace of another kind. It is peace that the world cannot give nor take away from you (see John 14:27). It should make the world envious of us.

Christians who are not experiencing this peace will not have an impact in the world as an influencer for Christ and His kingdom. It is difficult to engage in the word and ministry of reconciliation when you do not act like you have been reconciled to God (see 2 Corinthians 5:17-21). Christians who are not at peace contradict having peace with God. It is possible to have peace with God and not experience or express the peace of God. When we do not rest in peace with God, the peace of God is hindered by uncertainty. When we do not realize and accept that we have passed from death into life, the peace of God escapes us. When we do not rest in the fact that there is now no condemnation to those who are in Christ Jesus, the peace of God can elude us. When Christians fail to trust in the biblical promise of eternal life, that nothing can separate them from the love of God, the peace of God cannot be fully experienced. Also, Christians living in disobedience and sin cannot experience the peace of God. While living in disobedience and sin, the mind is not stayed on God; therefore, the peace of God cannot be ours (see Isaiah 26:3). When sin is temporarily ruling in the heart, there will be conviction and not peace. When the Spirit grieves because of unconfessed sins, saints are not able to experience God's peace. Thank God that this is true, for it is evidential of salvation (see 1 John 1:7–2:2). You are to be congratulated if you mourn over sin and experience no peace until your fellowship with God is restored (see Matthew 5:4).

Those who experience the peace of God will automatically become peacemakers (see Matthew 5:9). The presence of peacemakers in the world and in the church will certainly make a difference. Peacemakers have a peace presence. The character of a peacemaker is seen in the remainder of the graces of the fruit of the Spirit: patience, kindness, faithfulness, gentleness, and self-control. It is inconceivable that one can have the peace of God and be impatient, unkind, abusive, unfaithful, and reckless. A peaceful Christian will influence growth in the body of Christ.

We influence the world for Christ when we demonstrate *patience*. Patience is shown towards us in salvation (see 2 Peter 3:9; 1 Timothy 1:15, 16). Plus, patience inherent in the new birth is the impetus for our being patient with others. To be impatient with others is gracelessness. With patience, believers influence the world for salvation as they are tolerant and longsuffering under injuries inflicted upon them by others. Patience is a willingness to accept situations that are irritating and painful. To walk in the Spirit enables this kind of patience. As Christians, we do not seek to suffer, but when suffering comes upon us it is an act of the will not to respond in irritation. We are not designed to endure long-term suffering. We do not choose the path of patience or longsuffering whether it is within the body of Christ (see Ephesians 4:2; Colossians 3:12-15); in the world (see 2 Timothy 4:2-5; 1 Peter 2:18-25); or in the home (see 1 Peter 3:1-6). Therefore, a believer demonstrating patience is effectual because it is the work of the Holy Spirit through the believer. Patience is a matter of loving people (see 1 Corinthians 13:4). Peacemakers are patient. Where there is patience, there is a sense of grace. Patience is not tolerance. It is extending grace to the undeserved with full knowledge that the person is undeserving. Patient Christians are not obnoxious. The patient Christian understands God's longsuffering towards him (see 2 Peter 3:9). Patience is so much like God. Grace (as patience) demonstrated in believers in this age of hostility, retribution, haste, insensitivity, self-righteousness, and impatience has influential powers.

Christian *kindness* is another grace in the fruit of the Spirit that influences growth in the body of Christ. The kindness Jesus has towards us is an example (see Matthew 11:28, 29). It is His gentle and tender concern for us that we must express towards others (see 2 Timothy 2:24, 25). Kindness is purposeful; it carries the idea of usefulness on behalf of others. When we build up one another with words and deeds in loving kindness, onlookers become envious (see 1 Thessalonians 2:6-8). In an age where rudeness, harshness, crudeness, and greed are prevalent, kindness stands out as abnormal behavior. In an unkind world, Christian kindness is exemplary (see Ephesians 4:32). In this passage, kindness is expressed in forgiveness. When you release those who have been unkind to you, you also are kind to yourself. What is the difference between kindness and Christian kindness? Only Christians have experienced the kindness of God in Christ Jesus. What makes Christian kindness exceptional is that it is an expression in grace. It is kindness expressed towards the unkind, the unloving, and the undeserving. As it was expressed in Jesus (see Romans 5:6-8) so it is manifested in believers towards others.

The Old Testament example of Christian kindness is shown in David's kindness towards Mephibosheth (see 2 Samuel 9:1-13). The parable of the Prodigal Son is kindness exemplified (see Luke 15:11-32), and the parable of the Good Samaritan is another classic example of kindness (see Luke 10:29-37). Joseph's kindness expressed toward his unkind brothers is another example of Christian kindness (see Genesis 45:1-28). Christians are kind fundamentally because they have experienced kindness in Christ (see Titus 3:4, 5). Kindness is love in action (see 1 Corinthians 13:4). Jesus is the epitome of kindness. On the cross, Jesus demonstrated extreme kindness toward the unkind and the undeserving when He died in the place of sinners. An unkind Christian is a contradiction to the reality of the new birth. An unkind Christian grieves the Holy Spirit (see Ephesians 4:30-32). An unkind Christian is flavorless and ineffective (see Matthew 5:13-16). A kind Christian and church would be attractive in an unkind, ungraced, unforgiving world, influencing growth in the body of Christ. *What would I have if I had Jesus?* You would have Holy Spirit-produced kindness that is a response to God's kindness to you in Christ Jesus.

Christian *goodness* is another grace in the fruit of the Spirit that influences growth in the body of Christ. We are aware that God alone is intrinsically good (see Psalm 100:5; Nahum 1:7). So unlike humanity (see Romans 3:9-18), God is inherently good. There may be some seemingly positive attributes in people, but we are not intrinsically good. We do see the goodness in humanity in times of great peril and human atrocities. At times, even in the worst of us, we see goodness expressed. But goodness is not innate to humanity. It is not part of our essential nature and makeup. This is a hard truism for most people to accept. Humanity lobbies for a noble anthropology instead of owning its ignoble anthropology. What is innate to humanity is sin (see Psalm 51:5; Romans 5:12; Ephesians 2:3). People can do good, but we are not by nature good. The rich young ruler in his exchange with Jesus spoke of doing good deeds in order to have eternal life. Jesus informed him that only God was good (see Matthew 19:16, 17). Jesus qualified and defined good as intrinsic to the character of God. The rich young man was unaware that Jesus was the truth about God, therefore good. It is possible for people to do good without being good. But doing good can make one think she or he is good enough to please God. Herein lies self-righteousness—attempting to please God with one's works and perceived goodness (see Romans 10:1-4). Christian goodness flows from a believer's relationship with Jesus. Therefore, Christians can be good because of their new nature and do good because of the indwelling Holy Spirit (see Ephesians 2:10). Goodness as part of the Christian's character is Christ's life flowing through the Christian's towards others in the church and community (see Galatians 6:10). When this goodness is seen by the unbelieving world, it becomes influential (see 1 Peter 2:15-21). Christian goodness is a practical form of apologetics (see Titus 2:6-8). Through our goodness and good deeds we influence growth in the body of Christ.

Christian *faithfulness* is another grace in the fruit of the Spirit. To be faithful is so much like God. God is faithful towards us. He is a faithful Creator (see 1 Peter 4:19). He is faithful in the call (see 1 Corinthians 1:9; Romans 8:28-30). Those who are called shall be glorified. He is faithful in the midst of believers' temptations (see 1 Corinthians 10:13). He is faithful to forgive us (see 1 John 1:9). He is faithful to His promises (see Hebrews 10:23; 11:11). He is faithful in His protection (see 2 Thessalonians 3:3). Jesus is the faithful witness (see Revelation 3:14). Faithfulness is in the DNA of the new nature and is the birthmark of the new birth. Faithfulness characterizes believers, and when the believer is unfaithful he or she is acting out of character. Unfaithfulness contradicts faithfulness and is an insult to the faithfulness of God and grievous to the Holy Spirit. To be unfaithful is to be ungrateful to the faithfulness of Christ in salvation. Remember that the fruit of the Spirit is produced at salvation in every believer. In a world where faithfulness is rare, this grace is manifested through the Spirit and stands out and is thus considered unusual. This faithfulness is not simply being faithful to a task; it is the type of faithfulness that remains "in spite of." It is the type of faithfulness that can be backed up with the following words: "Although you slay me, I will remain allegiant to Christ" (see Job 13:15). It is faithfulness to an unbending worship of the true God (see Daniel 3:8-18; 6:10-23); a faithfulness that remains bold in the face of opposition (see Acts 3:13-20); a faithfulness that holds firm until death comes. It is a "finishing well" type of faithfulness (see 2 Timothy 4:6-8; Revelation 2:10). The grace of faithfulness is so fixated on the relationship with Jesus that the believer keeps pursuing Him (see Philippians 3:10), and if that same believer were to be unfaithful or cheat on Christ, their fixation drives them to ask for forgiveness and engage a process of repentance.

Peter cheated in his relationship with Christ by thrice denying Him, and Peter wept bitterly over his unfaithfulness (see Matthew 26:69-75). Faithfulness in the relationship says I will serve and have no other gods before the one I love. Unlike Gomer, Christians are to be faithful to

Christ. Gomer was unfaithful to her husband Hosea. The story told in the Old Testament book of Hosea was a practical, true-life, illustration of Israel's unfaithfulness to God. As terrible as the relationship was between Hosea and Gomer, and God and Israel, unfaithfulness is also prevalent in the relationship between Christ and Christians today. For when we sin as Christians, it is adulterous behavior. It is sin against the believer's relationship with Christ. A sinful Christian is an ineffective Christian. He or she cannot influence growth in the body of Christ while living in sin. Faithful obedience in the relationship is necessary to prevent infidelity in the relationship with Christ. We win when each member grows in relationship with Jesus; therefore, when one member of the body sins, it affects the whole body (see 1 Corinthians 5:1-13). Faithfulness is germane to the new birth. Infidelity is not germane to the new nature. Faithfulness, although a grace quality produced in us by the Holy Spirit, cannot be faithfully demonstrated in us without the believer's faithfully walking in the Spirit and being filled with the Spirit (see Galatians 5:16-24; Ephesians 5:18).

Christian *gentleness* or *meekness* is another grace of the fruit of the Spirit. It is often misunderstood as weakness when, in reality, meekness is strength under control and is produced in the believer by the Holy Spirit during regeneration. It is operative in the believer when the Holy Spirit controls the believer. The believer cannot take credit for the manifestation of meekness in his or her life. When we were sinners we were untamed, and then we met Jesus the wild-man tamer (see Mark 5:1-20). He called us into the kingdom of meekness (see Matthew 11:28-30). He broke the spirit of rebellion deep within, and by faith we surrendered to His will, thus becoming tame. Tamed Christians influence growth in the body of Christ. In meekness we surrendered to the Gospel of Christ (see Ephesians 1:13; 2 Thessalonians 1:8). The act of obedience to the Gospel is an act of meekness. This is what occurred in the life of the apostle Paul, formerly Saul, the great persecutor of Christians and the Lord's church. He was tamed on the road to Damascus and turned from being a persecutor to being a preacher of the Gospel (see Acts 9:3-6, 11-19, 22). The Lord broke Saul in order to produce a tamed Paul. The Lord did not destroy Paul's manhood, but instead He transposed his manhood into the kingdom of His Son.

Grace through faith tenderizes and transforms the believer into a gentle giant. Jesus said, *"Blessed are the meek"* (Matthew 5:5). Meek and gentle Christians are self-controlled. In what sense are the meek to inherit the earth? This has not been clearly delineated by interpreters, but it may have reference to the Christian's influence on earth. Disciplined strength is not unique to Christians. We find this quality in other religions and unbelievers in general. Christian strength in subjection influences growth in the body of Christ because of its difference. It operates under the rule and power of the kingdom of God. The kingdom of God comes to earth through Christian meekness. Both Jesus and Moses had meek beginnings, and deliverance was the result (see Numbers 12:3; Matthew 11:29).

Paul spoke of strength in weakness (see 2 Corinthians 12:10). Jesus died in weakness (see 2 Corinthians 13:4) but lived in power. Power is found in self-denial, a form of meekness (see Luke 9:23, 24). God can do more with us and through us when we are weak (see 2 Corinthians 12:9, 10). *"What would I have if I had Jesus?"* You would have strength in weakness because God is glorified in our weakness.

The final grace in the fruit of the Spirit is Christians *under control.* As meekness is strength under control, temperance is self under control, or self-mastery. Christians who manifest this grace are self-disciplined in body, soul, and spirit. This grace produces moderation in that which is good and abstinence of all that the Bible declares that is unrighteous. Self-control is a supernatural quality in the Christian. Self-control for the Christian is self being controlled by the Spirit. A self-controlled Christian is an antithesis to the work of the flesh. Walking in the Spirit keeps us under the Spirit's control. Where there is no self-control, there is no walking in the Spirit.

We are apt to perform the works of the flesh when we are left to ourselves. When we are not acting Christ-like, great distain is heaped upon us. Not being Christ-like is either a matter of being unrelated to Jesus or not being filled with the Spirit (see Romans 8:9-11; Ephesians 5:18). The enemy of Christ wants us to live in contradiction to who we are in Christ. Those who accuse us of not being Christian are unaware of the struggle between the flesh and spirit. At times, we as Christians fall short of being and doing like Jesus. Christians have a misunderstanding of self-control if they believe that it is self-produced. Christians are not the source of self-control rather the object of self-control.

Influential Christians enable growth in the body of Christ—new growth, not transplant growth. Influential Christians become believable witnesses to the power of the Gospel of salvation. They do not perjure themselves on the witness stand in the world's court. The case for Christ is not thrown out for a lack of evidence. When arrested for being and doing like Jesus, the evidence is so obvious that the jury is unanimous in their verdict; there is no split in the vote, no hung jury. Guilty as charged, they are Christians. Influential Christians are not obnoxious, but obviously who they purport to be. Therefore, they are not obstacles to the faith. Let me leave this point with a sobering word. Being influential does not mean everyone in your concentric circle of influence will be influenced for Christ. Their lack of response to the Gospel should not be due to our non-representation of Christ in the world (see Romans 2:24; 1 Peter 2:12). We are left in the world to put a good taste in the mouths of lost men and women for the sake of Christ. Relational evangelism is the divine stratagem for new growth in the body of Christ. It must become the backdrop for verbally sharing the Gospel.

The Salt and Light Factors

The mystery and the miracle of life and eternal life render us mere bystanders and agents in the grand scheme of life. Man is not the principal actor in either life or eternal life; he is a participant. It is the Creator and the Redeemer that is solely responsible for life and eternal life (see Acts 17:28; John 10:28). In the great drama of salvation, the believer is at best a member of the supporting cast. The stars in God's drama of salvation are the Son of Man and the Holy Spirit. In actuality, we are not soul winners. Proverbs 11:30 is not commending us to win souls, but to take hold of, capture, or value life. It is saying do not waste life. We really do not bring people to Christ; they are drawn to Christ by the convicting work of the Holy Spirit (see John 16:5-15). The mystery and the miracle of eternal life are of God and Him alone. The new birth into eternal life is totally supernatural in origin (see John 3:1-15). The Father who sent the Son draws the sinner (see John 6:44). The Father draws sinners through the redemptive activity of the Savior (see John 3:14-16; 12:32, 33). Please note that believing in Jesus Christ as Savior includes our birthing into the kingdom of God (see John 3:1-21). Our part in the drama of redemption is essentially influential in nature. As salt and light in the world we influence new growth in the body of Christ. We are not responsible for changing people. We are not responsible for winning people. We are simply responsible for influencing people. The power of salt and light is in their presence. The power is in the nature of the salt and light. The purpose of both is to *be* salt and to *be* light.

In this chapter, I have attempted to stress the importance of Christian character in effecting new growth in the body of Christ. It is primarily through our ontological witness that we participate in the drama of redemption. Before we participate in sharing the word of reconciliation, the word must become flesh. The power of the word of reconciliation is the evidence that we have been reconciled (see 2 Corinthians 5:17-21). As ambassadors of Christ, we represent the reconciled community in an unreconciled world. Perhaps the ministry of reconciliation that precedes the word of reconciliation is our serving the world as salt and light. As salt and light, we are being like Jesus who is the Light of the world (see John 8:12). We are also reflectors of His light like John the Baptist (see John

1:6-13). Paul described believers as children of light and children of the day living in the darkness of night (see 1 Thessalonians 5:5-8). Our influence is borne out of our being Christ's workmanship (see Ephesians 2:10). We are most effective in the world when we are who Christ has recreated us to be. We are His poetry, His workmanship, and His masterpiece in a world of godlessness. Christian presence is to influence righteousness in a crooked and perverse world. We are to be light in the midst of crookedness and perversion (see Philippians 2:12-15). The church of Jesus Christ must influence and challenge the moral consciousness of the world and nation. As members of the prophetic community, believers must speak truth to the powers that be. We must remember and rest in the assurance that we are not alone in this task because the Holy Spirit is with us and His power is available in us (see John 14:15-18; Philippians 2:12, 13). The supernatural life and ministry of the believer requires the supernatural presence and power of the Holy Spirit. If the Christian life and ministry seems to be out of reach, that is because it is. Jesus' purpose is for us to be and do what we cannot be and do without Him. We can be and do nothing without Him (see John 15:5; Philippians 2:12, 13). Our boast must be centered on the Lord. It is His Spirit that makes the Christian life exceptional (see Zechariah 4:6; Ephesians 6:10).

We also influence growth in the body of Christ by glorifying God. This is living out the human purpose. Humanity was created in the image of God to reflect His glory in the earth. Due to sin, humankind has fallen short of His glory (see Romans 3:23). Through the new birth this glory lost in the first Adam is restored through the Second Adam, Jesus Christ. In sanctification the believer is being transformed into the image of God, from glory to glory (see 2 Corinthians 3:18). The destiny of the believer is to be like Jesus (see Romans 8:29). Our destiny is not personal, but germane to every believer (see 1 John 3:1-3). We desire to grow in our relationship with Jesus in order to be like Him. Christ in us is the assurance of fully expressing God's glory (see Colossians 1:27). To reflect God's glory in the world is for the purpose of influencing growth in the body of Christ (see Ephesians 1:5-14). This glorifying presence is for the purpose of Jesus' name and is exclusively in the believer, by the grace of God, because Christ lives in the believer (see 2 Thessalonians 1:12). As believers we do not share Christ's glory; we simply reflect His glory (see Isaiah 48:11).

There is a correlation between being light and reflecting Christ's glory. Jesus is the light of the world. We are lesser light. He is the sun, we are the moon. The glory of the sun shines on the moon, giving the moon a reflective purpose. As believers, we do not make the light shine; we merely let it shine. We can hide the light, but we cannot make the light shine. The believer's light is innate to the new birth. To give God glory is much more than giving Him credit. It is to represent Him in the earth (see 2 Thessalonians 2:13, 14). Praising Him is cheapened when it is only with our mouths. We are called to praise Him with our lives. Praising God with music and instruments and not speaking well of Him with our behavior hinders our influence of growth in the body of Christ.

The call to evangelize the community and world can be frustrating when we fail to understand that the best we can do is influence. We are not called to invite sinners to attend our church as much as we are called to be so inviting that they would desire to surrender to Christ. The work of the church is in the world. Christ sends His church into the world as salt, light, ambassadors, and witnesses to influence sinners to surrender to Jesus Christ as Lord. The world is not to come to church; the church is called to go into the world being the Gospel and preaching the Gospel (see Matthew 28:19, 20).

Think It Through

1. Describe the pragmatic strategy for evangelism.

2. Name some ways that the Christian can answer the provocative question.

3. The influential power of the Christian life is the result of what?

4. What is meant by growth in the body of Christ?

5. Explain relational evangelism.

6. What is the fruit of the Spirit as it relates to the believer?

7. On what basis does God accept our demonstrations of love?

8. What are the salt and light factors that influence growth in the body of Christ?

9. What is required to have a supernaturally influential life?

CHAPTER

7

Influencing Maturity in the Body of Christ

*"We win when each member grows in relationship with Jesus, being, doing, thinking like Him, influencing growth and **maturity in the body of Christ**."*

As Christians, members of the body of Christ, the best thing we can do is influence growth and maturity. We certainly cannot produce growth and maturity, but we can nurture growth and maturity by cooperating with the work of the Spirit. We influence growth in the body through evangelism. We influence maturity through equipping, exhorting, and encouraging members in the body to grow up in Christ (see Ephesians 4:11-16). This passage defines what it means to be influential in the growth of the body of Christ.

Body Growth through Body Life

The prehistoric Christ was the Word in the beginning with God (see John 1:1, 2). The historic Christ was the Word that became flesh and dwelt among us (see John 1:14). The post-historic Christ is the church, His body on earth (see Ephesians 5:30; Colossians 1:18). The growth of each member of the body is for the sake of the whole. The baptism of the Holy Spirit places us in relationship with one another for the sake of body life. The maturation process, building up of one another in love, presents to the world one Christ. Christ created the church to be His presence on the planet after His ascension. Individual Christians and congregations must grasp this truth and engage in making it a reality. There is only one church of Christ, with many members and congregations. I am not speaking of the Church of Christ as a denomination, rather the church of Christ universal. The church that Christ is building, that the gates of hell will not prevail against, is the universal church (see Matthew 16:18). It is the church that you do not join, but you are born and baptized into. Congregations will dissolve, but the body of Christ is eternal.

How can we present the one Christ to a godless age? The answer is found in the Ephesians 4:11-16 passage. There must be unity of the faith. We must embrace the essential body of truth concerning Jesus Christ. Through body life, members operating in their giftedness will experience maturity. Every member is endowed with a supernatural gift or gifts. They are gifted for the sole purpose of edifying the body of Christ. Gifts were not given for self-growth. They were given to influence maturity in the body of Christ. The private use of gifts was not the intent of the Giver (see 1 Corinthians 12:4-7). All of the gifts are designed to influence maturity in the body. Norman Kraus rightly said:

"The messianic mission belongs not to individuals as such, but to the community of witness. This essential point has often been overlooked in Protestant circles where the mission was interpreted as a ministry of individuals to individuals with little or no appreciation for the centrality of the church. The church, not the individual, is the body of Christ in mission. Individuals are members of the body, and the gifts of the Spirit are entrusted to them as resources for the mission of the body."[21]

Solo Christianity is not the Spirit's strategy for maturing saints for the sake of the developing a healthy body witness in the world. Body life and not individual life is the Spirit's strategy. We must understand this divine intent for believers to live out their purpose in community. The same thing that hindered the unity in the Corinthian church hinders the church today: the

---

21 C. Norman Kraus, The Authentic Witness (William B. Eerdmans Publishing Company, Grand Rapids, 1979), p.23.

misuse of gifts. Personal gifting was not for personal use but for the benefit of the whole. The church is not present in the world through individual Christians, but exclusively through Christ's body. The misuse of gifts in the Corinthians church was due to loveless behavior in the congregation. They were not demonstrating loving one another with their gifts. They were self-serving instead of serving one another (see 1 Corinthians 13:1-14:1; Galatians 5:13-15). When gifts are not used for the benefit of the body, but a badge of elitism, it causes dysfunction in the body. Love is the foundation of the fruit of the Spirit, and love is the focal point of the gifts of the Spirit. It is the impetus for ministering with gifts in the body. To say you love God but do not demonstrate love towards members of the body is unnatural to the new life in the believer (see 1 John 3:10-18). We are called to lay down our lives as an expression of love. It ought to be a small matter to use our gifts for the sake of members in the body of Christ. Each member is called to influence maturity in the body of Christ. We do so with the proper use of gifts in the context of love. Let us look at some of the gifts to see how they influence maturity in the body of Christ.

Apostle and Prophet

Apostles and prophets were gifts to the church. According to Ephesians 4:11, they were gifts and they had gifts. They were the foundational gifts to the church (see Ephesians 2:20). These men were not simply foundational gifts because they formed the first core of believers (see Mark 16:17-18). Neither were they foundational in the sense that the church rested upon them, no! It is clear that Jesus is the Chief Cornerstone on which the church rests (see 1 Peter 2:6-8). The apostles were men who had been with Jesus, who were directly commissioned by Jesus, and uniquely authorized by Him. They were eyewitnesses of the resurrected Jesus (see 1 Corinthians 9:1, 2; 15:1-9). What they taught became the basic tenets of the faith (see Acts 2:42). The manifestation of signs and wonders confirmed the authenticity of the apostles (see 2 Corinthians 12:11, 12). Some associates of the apostles also performed signs and wonders (see Luke 10:1-9; Acts 6:8; 8:6). With the primary apostles, the manifestation of signs and wonders ceased. The foundational gifts were established and verified with the sign gifts. These primary apostles influenced and effected maturity in the body of Christ through receiving and recording the revealed Word of truth. What they said and wrote concerning Jesus Christ is the literary foundation on which Christian faith and practice stands. In this age, there can only be apostles in the secondary sense—missionaries and church planters. There is a distinction between the apostles of Christ and the apostles of the church. Being sent by Christ is different from being sent by the church (see Acts 11:23). Apostles in the secondary capacity are missionaries establishing the Lord's work where there was no Christian presence (see Romans 15:20). The missionary function of the apostles has been and still is impactful and influential in maturing the body of Christ.

The same is true of the prophets. There are no prophets in the primary sense in the contemporary church, only in the secondary sense. The prophets of old influenced maturity in that they unfolded the mind of God. God spoke directly to them, and they spoke directly to the people the words of God. They received direct revelation from the Lord. Before there were written texts of Scripture that served as literary guides, the prophets were gifts from God granted direct revelation. We notice this gift in men like Mark, Luke, James, and Jude. Prophets did more explaining, while apostles did more proclaiming of the truth. There was some foretelling, but mostly there was forthtelling. The prophets influenced maturity in the body of Christ by expounding on the revelation from the Lord. As foundations to the early church they were God's spokesmen and penmen of the Word of God (see Ephesians 3:1-7; 2 Peter 1:20, 21; Jude 3). These first witnesses who walked with Jesus impacted and influenced the church in its maturity. These inspired men were special in that they received the inspiration of Scripture from the Holy Spirit (see 2 Timothy 3:16).

The prophets today can only be preachers, forthtellers speaking from the sacred Scriptures. They are illumined at best but certainly not inspired. Jesus Christ, the revealed Word of God is the final revelation of God (see Hebrews 1:1-4). There can be no new revelations if Jesus is the final revelation of God. Jesus is the first and the last Word from God (see John 1:1, 14; Revelation 3:14). The influence of the apostles and prophets is found in their skeletal and foundational contribution to the health of the body of Christ. The church today must do like the early church if we are to be healthy. *"And they continued steadfastly in the apostle's doctrine and fellowship, in the breaking of bread, and in prayers"* (Acts 2:42).

Evangelist

These Christians are the pioneer gifts to the church. They have the spiritual ability to communicate the Gospel in relevancy. They influence new growth in the body of Christ. You cannot have maturation without first having life—no new life, no maturity of life. Evangelism is the business of the entire church, but there are those within the church who are evangelists with the special spiritual ability to explain and express the Gospel message in such a digestible manner that it results in a salvation response. So the evangelist is used of the Spirit as an obstetrician, delivering the baby. The pastor/teacher is used of the Spirit as a pediatrician, nurturing the baby.

Pastor/Teacher

The pastor/teacher is the key influencer in the body of Christ. He is responsible for spiritual maturation through the preaching and teaching ministry of the church (see Acts 20:28, 29; 1 Peter 5:1, 2). He influences maturity through proclamation and explanation of the Word of God, but also through demonstration. He takes the oversight of the church as an apologist and example to the flock (see 1 Peter 5:3). Someone rightly said that leadership is influence. Goats and cows are driven, but sheep must be led. I have met many pastors who believe in a leadership style of being a driver instead of a shepherd. Shepherds lead and they do it primarily as examples to the flock. Shepherds must smell like the sheep. They live among the sheep (see 1 Peter 5:1-4). It is difficult to know what to feed them if one does not live among them. Shepherds are not hirelings. It is not the money; it is the calling. They are not mercenaries but ministers. The sheep do not belong to the shepherd, but to the Good Shepherd who laid down His life for them (see John 10:11-18). As he cares for the sheep, the shepherd is constantly reminded of his own sheepish nature. He realizes that he is a sheep called out to be shepherd. God's Son became like us to experience human life and to expiate for human sins. The pastor lives among the sheep to tend to their needs in the process of sanctification.

The pastor/teacher influences maturity in that he aids in restoring the saints to God's original purpose for humanity. The equipping ministry of the pastor/teacher is one of setting broken bones. The perfecting or the completing of the saints is moving them towards being, doing, and thinking like Jesus. Through preaching and teaching the body of Christ is being built up into one perfect bride. This is the means in which the entire body is matured through the Word of God (see 1 Peter 1:22-2:3). Individual members of the body of Christ mature for the sake of the maturity of the whole body. The pastor is the key influencer of the process of spiritual maturation of the body of Christ. The influencing of maturity in the body is in order that Christ may be present through His church in the world. The purpose of the church on earth is to be the reincarnation of Jesus or the extension of the incarnation of Jesus on earth. The Holy Spirit has become responsible for another earthly body of Christ to dwell in the earth. As the Spirit is responsible for Jesus' incarnation, so He is responsible for Jesus' reincarnation. The historical Jesus is the result of the Holy Spirit. He is also the One who places or baptizes believers into the body of Christ, forming the post-historic Christ, the church (see Matthew 1:20; 1 Corinthians 12:13).

The man of God, not with his credentials, charisma, and craft, but fundamentally through his character (see 1 Timothy 3:1-7; Titus 1:5-9) is pivotal in outfitting the church to become the extension of the incarnation of Christ. One day, he must give an account to the Chief Shepherd of how he has functioned as the key influencer of the incarnation, growth, and maturity of the Body of Christ (Hebrews 13:17).

Make Disciples

The pastor's task is to make disciples. The last thing Jesus said to His disciples was to make disciples (see Mathews 28:19, 20). The last thing ought not be the least thing the church does. Jesus' priority must become ours. Our agenda must be His agenda. It is His church. He purchased the church with His blood (see Acts 20:28). He is head of His church (Colossians 1:18). Therefore, since He died for the church and is head of the church, He has the authority and right to command its purpose in the world. *"All authority in heaven and in earth has been given to me. Go therefore and make disciples of all nations, baptizing them in the name of the Father and of the Son and of the Holy Spirit, teaching them to observe all that I have commanded you. And behold, I am with you always, to the end of the age"* (Matthew 28:18b-20, ESV). This is the imperative: make disciples.

What does it mean to make a disciple? The profundity of the phrase "make disciples" has been simplified to the idea of learner or follower. Jesus did not define discipleship. He described the discipleship process in how He related and interacted with His disciples. Jesus related to His disciples, revealing the Father and reproducing Himself in and through His disciples. Thus, a disciple is an obedient follower of Jesus, relating, reflecting, and reproducing disciples. A disciple is not a mere follower and learner. It is more profound than one who follows the teachings of a teacher. Jesus dwelt among His disciples (see John 1:14), revealing the Father to them (see John 14:8), and reproduced Himself in them (see John 14:18-24). Disciple-makers influence maturity in the body of Christ. Through evangelism believers are added to the body of Christ. But through disciple-making, believers are multiplied into the body. According the Great Commission strategy, multiplication is Jesus' intended method of growing His church. The natural means of populating the earth is through reproduction, so it is spiritually. The church grows best through reproduction. Growth by means of addition is better than nothing, but growth through multiplication is healthier. Children grow up best in a parental environment. Spiritual children grow up healthier in a spiritual parental environment. Discipleship is Jesus' process of influencing maturity in the body of Christ. It is developmental in nature, nurturing spiritual infants into spiritual parents. The goal in discipleship is every member of the body of Christ becoming a disciple-maker.

In the discipleship process, there are the four Ms: make, mark, mature, and multiply disciples. We notice this in Matthew 28:19, 20; there is the injunction to *make* disciples, *mark* them in baptism, *mature* them by teaching, and in 2 Timothy 2:2 Paul instructs *multiplication* reproduction. The fact that baptism follows making disciples in the Great Commission suggests that disciples become disciples in the new birth. A disciple is not different from a believer. All believers are disciples, called to make disciples of all ethnicities. Disciples make disciples. Disciples of Christ are more than fans and mere followers. They are disciplined followers of Christ who have denied themselves and taken up their crosses, and they follow Him daily (see Luke 9:23-27).

The win statement speaks of growing in relationship with Jesus, but we also grow in relationship with one another in the body of Christ. This indispensable union in the body necessitates investing in the lives of other members in the body. If we are to effect maturity in the body each member must mature in relationship with one another. Discipleship requires investing in the lives of unbelievers and new believers. The Great Commission and the Great Commandment (see John 13:34, 35) must become the impetus for investing in others. Christ sends us into the world and places us in the church to invest in the lives of others. To make and mature disciples requires being inconvenienced. Discipleship is influenced when the disciple-maker is growing in his or her relationship with Jesus, being, doing and thinking like Jesus. When the unbeliever and the new believer are exposed to a disciple-maker's influence a discipleship atmosphere is created. When discipleship is viewed merely as evangelism and Christian education, we have only partially obeyed the Great Commission. It must include what was demonstrated by Jesus: relating, reflecting/revealing, and reproducing disciples. Discipleship must be comprehensive in nature, affecting the whole man—body, soul, and spirit.

New member classes have been a blessing to the church. They have orientated new members and Christians into the teachings and life of the congregation. But for discipleship to really take place, the teacher must become a disciple-maker, sharing life with the student. The teacher must make an influential investment beyond the classroom encounter. For reproduction to happen a relationship with the student is expedient in order for the student to be exposed to the new life in the teacher (see 2 Timothy 2:2). It is not reasonable to think this can happen where there is one disciple-maker and several students. Jesus had twelve disciples, and at times three whom He brought closer to Him (see Matthew 17:1, 2). Discipleship takes place best where there is intimacy.

The Family and Discipleship

The family is the primary, fundamental institution. God created and established the family before He did any other structures. This was not coincidental. The Creator had purpose in the primacy of the family. The family predates the Temple, the synagogue, and the church. The fact of the family's primacy suggests its foundational purpose in human society. Church and other institutions are comprised of families. The health of society is essentially connected to the health of the families. So it is with the church. However, the church does not appear to be family-friendly. The church that does not view the family as the primary place to make disciples is probably either in a parasitic or competitive relationship with the family. It exists either at the expense of the family, or it operates in an unfriendly manner towards the family. The cooperative church with it family events and marriage ministries, though good, is not the best. Thank God for family emphasis and family ministries, but seeing the family as the ministry in the church is far better. The Christian family becomes the primary place to make disciples when the family and church functions in a symbiotic relationship. The church must be more than para-family, and the family must be more than parachurch. The church and the Christian family are one and the same. How we view the family is crucial. It must be viewed as the ministry of the church and not a ministry, a mere auxiliary or department of the church. The primacy that God places on the family demands that it should be the ministry of the church.

The rules of baseball illustrate the importance of the family. If the baserunner fails to touch first base but touches second, third, and home plate, the umpire declares the runner out at home plate. The Christian family is first base, and the church can be seen as second base. The church has been guilty of failing to touch first base. What the church does after missing first base is not as effectual as it could be on second base. Our social ills and the church's unhealthiness are family related. The Christian parent is a disciple-maker. The spiritual, mental, and emotional health of the husband and wife will determine the health of the marriage and family. As the couple enters the sanctity of marriage the divine purpose of the holy institution must be understood. The first thing the couple needs to realize is that marriage is God's idea. Adam and Eve did not ask to be married. It was God's plan for His purpose. Secondly, marriage is godly, designed for godly people. The ungodly cannot live out God's purpose for marriage on earth. Thirdly, marriage is for God's purpose and glory. Marriage is not primarily for the couple, but for God's use. Marriage belongs to God, and the godly couple is a steward of the institution. For the marriage to be pleasing to God it must function in godliness. Godliness begins with God's design for marriage (see Genesis 1:27, 28; 2:18, 21-25), which is marriage between a male and a female. The idea of marriage presupposes opposites becoming one. There can be no marriage between the same; you cannot marry yourself. You cannot have two males marry or two females marry and call that a marriage. This is not according to God's design. Since God designed it, He has all authority to define it. You and I have no authority to redefine what the Designer has defined as holy matrimony. When people tamper with marriage, the holy becomes unholy. In these days, there is a divorcement from God's design that causes me to declare, "What God has joined together, let no one separate (Matthew 19:6, NIV). God has not purposed to join two men or two women together in unholy matrimony. A holy God cannot identify with the unholy. Yes! God is love, but His love never contradicts His holiness (see 1 John 5:3).

The basic command to godly parents is to propagate the earth with children who bear the restored image of God. Godly parents are multipliers through procreation. The purpose of God in creation is for humankind to reflect His image. Godly parents, unlike good parents, communicate to their children the image of God. As disciple-making parents, they are influential in passing on the faith to the next generation so their children can also become image bearers. Godly parents are distinct from good parents in that, above all else, they desire their children to be like Jesus (see Galatians 4:19). The most lasting legacy a parent could leave children is a godly image. This would best influence spiritual maturity in children. Parents influence their children through their walk with God more than their work for God. Parents cannot force children to be godly. You can only influence godliness through your walk with God. That is what Adam and Eve did. Abel and Seth were godly but Cain was not (see Genesis 4:1-16, 25, 26). The goal and purpose of godly parents are to pass on God's image and likeness to the next generation (see Genesis 5:1-5). Parental discipleship is an awesome responsibility. It is like building an Ark for the saving of the household (see Hebrews 11:7). Noah's walk with God influenced his family to trust God's provision of salvation—the Ark. The father and mother's walk with God should strongly influence the children to trust in the Christ of salvation. And it should affect the children to mature in the faith in order to pass on the legacy to their children. Parental discipleship is like fruit-bearing (see John 15:8). Christian character is influential to bearing fruit inside the family.

Faith lived out in the home is important to making disciples. The work of the church is a continuation of the work in the home. Faith practiced and taught at home is primetime discipleship. It is both quantitative and qualitative time. In the average family most of the span of time is experienced at home, and the nature of the relationships determines the quality of time, especially in a caring and loving environment. Therefore, the godly home is invaluable for making disciples. Fathers and mothers are progenitors, providers, and protectors, but also prophets and priests. As prophets they are God's voices in the home, and as priests they are the family's voices before the throne of God. Although Adam failed, he was God's voice and intercessor in the Adam's family (see Genesis 3:8-24). God's design and purpose is for the man to be the spiritual leader in the home. This is obvious in the first family. Adam was the responsible person, and his irresponsibility affected the entire human race (see Romans 5:12-14). Adam's failure did not cause God to change leadership in the family. God called Adam into accountability by asking him where he was in his role as leader (see Genesis 3:9), but He did not fire him as leader of the family. God's sending the Second Adam is the ultimate proof that He did not given up on the man as leader. The apostle Paul understood that husbands were a valuable part of God's strategy for fulfilling His purpose in and through the family (see 1 Corinthians 11:2-12; Ephesians 5:22-33).

The Pauline letters are constantly under attack in this age because of the divine assignment of headship given to the husband and father. There are those inside and outside the church who question the trustworthiness of the Bible because of the idea of paterfamilias. But it is biblically clear that the sovereign Lord intends for godly men to take the point in the family. It is the role of responsibility, not privilege and preeminence. It is really more a servant's function than a superior status (see Ephesians 5:23). The essence of love is being inconvenienced for the sake of God's best for another. This is what the husband is called to do: give himself for the wellbeing of his wife. The husband is not the master of the home, rather he is the model in the home of what it means to be godly. He is essentially the spiritual example in the home. Jesus' headship is certainly authoritative, but a husband's headship is for influencing spiritual maturity in the home. Christ is Lord of the church and the home. The husband serves as steward of that which Christ is owner. He is not to rule his wife, he is to love and serve his wife of whom he is a steward for the Owner. It is the ungodly husband who rules over his wife (see Matthew 20:25-28). After the fall of Adam and Eve, the marriage was cursed with the idea of rulership (see Genesis 3:16). The poetic relationship, *"bone of my bones and flesh of my flesh"* was blurred by marital tension.

The significance of the man is seen in the divine and demonic focus. The enemy focuses on that which God prioritizes. The devil and his demons are after men whom God has purposed to take the point, the leadership in the home. We see this in the attempt to annihilate the male babies in Egypt (see Exodus 1:15-22), and the attempt to massacre all the male babies in the regions of Bethlehem (see Matthew 2:16-18). Although men are complicit, the attack of the enemy on men is evidential in their absence in the home and church and presence in prisons on street corners, or preoccupied with making money, reaching for the so-called American dream. The attack of the enemy speaks to the significance of men. If you want to know where the church needs to focus, observe where and on whom Satan is focusing. No wonder Jesus challenged His disciples to fish for men (see Matthew 4:19). We must not rush to make the challenge impersonal. I believe He meant men and not men and women. Jesus was prioritizing men as His focus of making and maturing disciples. Get the man and you have a better chance of influencing the whole household for Christ. The home desperately needs a Joshua-type husband and father who can speak boldly with a declarative statement pertaining to their families, *"As for me and my house, we will serve the Lord"* (Joshua 24:15b). Joshua, as husband and father, had influence.

If the home is to be the primary place to make disciples, affecting the health of the church, the Joshua-type father must be present, willing, and responsible in order to influence the next generation. If our children are to influence their generation and the next for Christ, then parents, children, and youth leaders must function as disciple-makers, relating, reflecting, and reproducing disciples (see 2 Timothy 2:2). The home and the church must be safe places for believers to become who they are in Christ Jesus. Atmospheric discipleship must cultivate an environment that influences maturity in the body of Christ. Healthy parents in healthy marriages or singleness, and healthy church leaders in healthy relationships are crucial for cultivating an environment that influences maturity in the body of Christ. When parents, pastors, and leaders contradict righteousness, spiritual influence is greatly impaired. Atmospheric discipleship is created in an environment of grace. A grace environment is where believers live in community with a keen sense of undeserved favor extended to them in God's grace. A graceless, legalistic, self-righteous atmosphere will make the church and home an unsafe environment, impeding spiritual maturity. In a grace culture, forgiveness is experience. Forgiveness, repentance, and restoration create a healthy environment that influence maturity. Failure in a grace environment is not viewed as final. It does not seek to abuse grace in order to continue in sin (see Romans 6:1), rather an appreciation of grace that mourns over personal sins (see Matthew 5:4). A Christian community where sin is celebrated and tolerated must not be viewed as grace. Discipline is germane to creating a grace environment (see Galatians 6:1-5). Unconfessed sins and undisciplined saints do not create an atmosphere in the church or home that is healthy (see 1 Corinthians 5:1-13). A church and home that tolerates sin will not be a safe place for believers to become who they are in Christ Jesus. A judgmental church or home have equally negative effects on maturity in the body of Christ. With the quest not to be judgmental, the church and home must not allow sinful behavior to be a way of life. A safe place to become who we are in Christ Jesus is a place where sanctification is taking place. The church and home must be sanctified places for the purpose of moving believers from regeneration towards glorification (see 1 John 3:1-3).

Atmospheric discipleship happens in a loving environment. When the church and home love one another in community, discipleship is enabled. Jesus said, *"By this all will know that you are My disciples, if you have love for one another"* (John 13:35, NKJV). A loving church and a loving home are powerful influences in the process of maturity in the body of Christ.

The Spiritual Gifts

We have already discussed the gifted men past and present that were and are influential in the maturation of the body of Christ. Gifts are given by the Holy Spirit to every member of the body of Christ is for the maturation of the whole body. Spiritual gifts are purposed by the Holy Spirit to influence maturity.

The Speaking Gifts

The Holy Spirit has purposed that the speaking gifts influence maturity in the body of Christ. The gift of *prophesy* (see 1 Corinthians12:10) is the spiritual gift of forth-telling. At this point in history the church is proclaiming revealed truth. It is proclaiming it through the preaching gift.

The preacher does not reveal truth. He declares truth already revealed. He preaches the Word (see 2 Timothy 4:2), the written Word. He preaches not from the Word, but the Word. He is an interpreter of the Word of God and not a revealer (see Acts 8:30-35). The preaching of the Word of God is the primary means of influencing maturity in the body of Christ (see 1 Peter 1:22-2:3). Whether you are a preacher or teacher, the unfolding of biblical truth is critical to the growth and maturity of the body. Therefore, the truth handler, like a brain surgeon, must be extremely careful with truth (see 2 Timothy 10-17).

The twin gifts of *wisdom* and *knowledge* are needed to help influence maturity in the body of Christ. They both were primarily functional in the revelation of the Word of God prior to the written Word. However, in this biblical period of church life, wisdom and knowledge are gifts used in the interpretation of Scripture, not the revelation of Scripture. These gifts are manifested in the preacher and teacher, but more so in those who have given their lives to the training of pastors, preachers, and teachers. These scholars are dedicated and disciplined in understanding the languages in which the Bible was written. The gifts of wisdom and knowledge are found in most Bible colleges and seminaries. This is not saying that these are the only places where the gifts are operative. But wisdom and knowledge are most useful where church leaders are being equipped for the preaching, teaching, and counseling ministries in the body of Christ. Those who equip the equippers ought to possess these two gifts because the Spirit gives gifts according to His will and purpose, and He gives them proportionately. The manifestation of the same gift can be greater in one gifted person than in another (see 1 Corinthians 12:1-7). Because the sovereign Spirit gives gifts according to His will and purpose we must also be cognizant that the effects and results of gifts will not be the same. But all are for the common good of the body of Christ. So it is with the gifts of wisdom and knowledge. In certain members in the body, the spiritual abilities to handle the Word of truth will be manifested on a different level.

Nonetheless, at the foundation of all Christian teaching and preaching should be the gifts of wisdom and knowledge. Grasping the meaning of what the Bible says is essential to communicating truth. It is most important that those who deal with the human mind know the mind of God, "rightly dividing the Word of truth" (2 Timothy 2:15).

The gift of *teaching* is the ability to interpret and articulate the revealed truth of Scripture in a learnable fashion and form. It is the ability to take the mysteries of Scripture, make them manageable and digestible for the purpose of conforming the Christian to the image Christ. Teachers use cognitive learning to bring about incarnational growth and maturity. Preaching is proclamation, and teaching is explanation of the Word of truth for the purpose of influencing maturity in the body of Christ.

Wisdom is available to all Christians (see James 1:5), but there are those with the supernatural gift of *wisdom*. It is not a wisdom separated from Scripture and the Spirit of truth. It is not philosophical wisdom or scientific wisdom, rather spiritual wisdom. This wisdom comes from God and is contextualized in Scripture. It will not violate Scripture. The Holy Spirit gives certain believers through reading, observation, and interpretation the gift to apply truth discovered. It is not new truth, but truth discovered through the illumination and gifting of the Holy Spirit.

Now the gift of *knowledge* is the spiritual ability to communicate insights into truth revealed (see Ephesians 3:3-7; Colossians 1:26; 2:2; 4:3). Knowledge is the ability to perceive and systematize the mysteries of God's Word. The gift of wisdom is more the application of the perceived, systematized mysteries of God's Word. Both gifts influence maturity in the body of Christ by helping us to know and do the will of God for the sake of the functioning of the body of Christ.

The gift of *exhortation* (see Romans 12:8) is the supernatural ability to comfort, to encourage, to counsel, and to exhort the discomforted through the Word of God (see 2 Timothy 4:2). There is exhortation in preaching, but this gift is often exercised in less formal and public forums. It is often manifested in counseling (see 2 Corinthians 1:3-7; Hebrews 10:24, 25). It is the gift of coming alongside a member of the body of Christ to help by rightly dividing the Word of truth in relation to a member's situation (see Acts 11:22-26; 15:36-41). It is speaking truth in love (see Ephesians 4:15). It is a gift concerned with restoration of the fallen member (see Galatians 6:1, 2). Wisdom is certainly needed in the operation of this gift of exhortation. This gift is invaluable in influencing maturity in the body of Christ.

The Serving Gifts

Under *serving* gifts I have included: *leadership, administration, ministering, showing mercy, faith,* and *discernment.*

The gift of *leadership* (see Romans 12:8) serves the body of Christ, enabling maturity. First and foremost, leaders must see themselves as servants (see Matthew 20:20-28). Leaders are not influential when they do not model Jesus as servants. Wanting high seats and positions in the body of Christ creates an atmosphere of competition and conflict in the church. There can be no healthy maturation in such an atmosphere. Leaders that model taking a towel and washing feet create a healthy climate for growth (see John 13:5-17). To lead is to take the point and stand before. It is not merely presiding, but pioneering. It is not being over others, but becoming an underling. Leadership at its best is influence. People follow leaders, so if there is no one following you, you do not have the gift of leadership. The leader must understand his or her destination. I have asked Christian leaders to explain their destination; as a leader, where are you going? A leader needs to know the destination. It has become clear to me that our destiny is not just some day being with Jesus, but moreover it is becoming more like Jesus. Our destiny is not a place, it is a person (see Philippians 3:12-14; Colossians 1:28, 29). The fact that the qualifications for leaders in the church deal with one's character suggests that the destination is to be like Jesus. Leaders influence maturity in the body of Christ by serving as examples of being conformed to the image of Christ (see Romans 8:29).

The gift of *administration* (see 1 Corinthians 12:28) is similar to that of leadership. The leadership gift is more people-oriented, while administration is more task-oriented (see Numbers 11:16, 17; Acts 6:1-4). Persons with this gift assist in steering the ship in its predetermined destination (see Exodus 18:13-27). Administrators are not always as influential as leaders are, but their gift does influence maturity in the body of Christ. They free up the pastor/teacher to continue in the Word and in prayer. Those with the spiritual gift of administration prevent the church from being efficient in doing ministry ineffectively. They influence maturity in the body by keeping the church focused on the win.

The gift of *service* or *ministry* (see Romans 12:7) differs from the gift of helps, in that it is task-oriented. While every member is a servant, the spiritual gift of service goes beyond the service of the average member. Those who are gifted to serve often do so sacrificially. Humility accompanies the gift of service. When it comes to serving in the body, those with this gift have the mind of Christ (see Philippians 2:5-8). Like Jesus, they model service in the body of Christ (see John 13:5-17). They influence maturity through serving others in the body of Christ in a practical way. They stir up an atmosphere of serving in the body. Instead of self-serving, those with this gift practice self-sacrifice.

The gift of *showing mercy* (see Romans 12:8) is the spiritual gift of caring for the hurting. It is one of the serving gifts that deals with the marginalized, the maligned, the miserable, mistreated, misfortunate, and misrepresented inside and outside the congregation. Members with this gift engage the sick and suffering with more than sympathy. To show mercy is to act empathetically to relieve suffering. Those with the gift of mercy will run towards the leprosy colony. Many in the church from time to time will do acts of mercy, but those with the gift show mercy as a way of life. You find them in hospitals, prisons, rest homes, hospice care situations, drug and alcohol addiction recovery ministries, AIDS clinics, and blighted communities meeting needs. Those with this gift have an overwhelming sense of God's mercy shown towards them that causes them to be merciful. This gift influences maturity in the body of Christ through caring.

The gift of *faith* (see 1 Corinthians 12:9) influences maturity in the body of Christ. This faith is not saving faith or sanctifying faith (see Ephesians 2:8, 9; 2 Corinthians 5:7) but a special gift of faith that some have. It is an extraordinary gift of faith that serves the body of Christ. This gift of faith is mountain-moving type faith (see Numbers 13:30-33). The gift of faith is demonstrated in Caleb and Joshua, two of the twelve spies sent to spy out the land of Canaan. They had faith in the impossible. Although they were not convincing and the people rejected their confidence in the Lord's ability to give them the Promised Land, they did serve as influencers. This gift of faith is designed to inspire God-sized endeavors. Their optimism influences doing the inexplicable wherein God gets the glory. They challenge mediocrity in the church. They are adventurous visionaries, daring dreamers; they have a seemingly reckless faith. They believe God for big things. They are the heroes of faith found listed in Hebrews 11. They trust God in all circumstances. This gift serves the church in creating an atmosphere of the miraculous, expecting God to surprise them.

The gift of *discernment* (see 1 Corinthians 12:10) also influences maturity in the body of Christ. It serves the church by guarding the church from doctrinal error. It was certainly useful before the completion of the Bible. It functioned in relationship to the gift of prophecy. Christian apologists have the gift of discernment. They have the spiritual ability to rightly divide the revealed Word of God in order to defend the faith once for all delivered to the saints (see Jude 3,4). They can distinguish between truth and error. Biblical error is detrimental to the maturity of the saints in the body of Christ. The church can grow numerically without spiritual discernment, but it cannot mature without it. Church success can disguise health. When the church is busy counting members instead of weighing them, they have settled for immaturity. The gift of discernment serves to keep the church healthy. Every member should be taught to discern error, but the church desperately needs this gift (see Acts 20:28-32; 1 John 2:20-27; 4:1). A pastor cannot be an overseer without the gift of discernment. He oversees through his preaching, teaching, and demonstration of truth (see 1 Peter 5:1-3). Discernment is key to influencing maturity in the body of Christ.

The Supporting Gifts

The supporting gifts are comprised of the gifts of *helps, giving*, and *hospitality*. These gifts are instrumental in influencing maturity in the body of Christ.

The gift of *helps* (see 1 Corinthians 12:28) somewhat differs from the gift of service in that it is more people-oriented. The believer with the gift of helps shares another's load (see Romans 16:1, 2). This is its function in the body of Christ. Members working in supportive roles in the body characterize this gift. They are the unnoticed members of the body who work behind the scenes. What the apostle called the weak, less honorable, and unpresentable (see 1 Corinthians 12:22, 23) members of the body are probably these helpers. Often they are the unsung heroes of the church. They are members who do not seek praise or recognition. They just get joy in holding up others. Some view those who help as not spiritual, but without them the spiritual work would be ineffective. The gift of helps is a spiritual gift. It is Spirit-given and can be more Spirit-enabled than the visible and noticeable gifts. Paul in many of his letters mentioned the unknown heroes of the Gospel (see Romans 16:3-16; Corinthians

16:13-17). They labored with Paul in the Gospel; many of them were not preachers but helpers in the Gospel. Helpers are characterized in the actions of Aaron and Hur, holding up the arms of Moses as Joshua led the battle against the Amalekites (see Exodus 17:8-16). Those with the gift of helps do not need encouragement like the visibly gifted. Gifted helpers are internally encouraged. Those with this gift influence maturity in their supportive capacities more than is realized.

The gift of *giving* (see Romans 12:8) is the supernatural gift of sacrificial generosity. Every member of the body is called to give like Abel gave: the first, the fat, and by faith (see Genesis 4:4; Hebrews 11:4). However, those with this gift are unnoticed. They are usually generous, unassuming, and unpretentious. They quietly meet needs of members in the fellowship. They are grace givers, and encourage grace giving and sacrificial giving in the face of the impossible. Barnabas had the gift of giving (see Acts 4:36, 37). He was a well-off saint. However, the Macedonian saints who were poor manifested the gift of giving (see 2 Corinthians 8:1-7). Gifted givers are motivated by the grace of God shown through Jesus Christ. It is their attitude towards God, Christ, and His church that influences maturity in the body of Christ. It is not the amount of their giving but their love of God that inspires their giving that influences maturity.

Finally, the gift of *hospitality* (see 1 Peter 4:9, 10) is a supportive gift that influences maturity in the body of Christ. Members with this gift create a healthy atmosphere for spiritual maturity. They help to incorporate new members in the congregation. They have a welcoming attitude and demeanor. Hospitable members, along with those who disciple, have a tremendous effect in the preservation of the new fruit. Those with the gift entertain strangers like they are entertaining angels (see Hebrews 13:2). I believe that Romans 12:9-13 bespeaks the gift of hospitality. This gift will defrost a frigid church. I have experienced sitting in worship next to a block of ice; thank God for the gift of hospitality that warmed my spirit so I could worship and hear the Word of God without shivering to death.

Think It Through

1. How is Christ present in the world today?

2. Define the purpose of spiritual gifts in the body of Christ.

3. How did the gifted apostles and prophets influence maturity in the body of Christ?

4. How does the gifted evangelist influence maturity in the body of Christ?

5. How does the gifted pastor/teacher influence maturity in the body of Christ?

6. How do the speaking gifts influence maturity in the body of Christ?

7. How do the serving gifts influence maturity in the body of Christ?

8. How do the supporting gifts influence maturity in the body of Christ?

9. What constitutes selfishness in the body of Christ as it relates to maturity in the body of Christ?

EPILOGUE

The Good News Church

The church cannot become influential in the community where it resides when it is embroiled in scandal. Churches that settle conflict in the world's court are ineffective witnesses. It is obvious that churches and Christians are targets of the enemy, but the church and Christians ought not to become complicit with the enemy. Conflict is not new to the church and Christians, but conflict should be handled biblically. When the world and its court systems are invited into the affairs of the body of Christ, its witness is greatly diminished (see 1 Corinthians 6:1-11). The church and the Christian render themselves powerless when they make the evening news because of misrepresentation. The Good News church ought not to become a bad news church because of scandalous and scathing behavior of leaders and members (see 1 Peter 4:12-19). If we are to influence maturity, Christ's church must be a place of deliverance, not drama.

A Sense of One Another

Influencing maturity in the body of Christ happens when each member grows spiritually mature. Individual growth is crucial to body life and growth (see Ephesians 4:13). This verse refers to corporate growth. John MacArthur said it this way, *"The church in the world is Jesus in the world, because the church is now the fullness of His incarnate body in the world."*[22] That fullness is in progress, but only present in the church, the only body of Christ on earth. This is why it is imperative that each member grow in relationship with Jesus, being, doing, thinking like Him, influencing growth and maturity in His body. Refusal to grow as a member of the body of Christ is a selfish act of disobedience. It impedes the whole body of Christ. This indispensable union makes individual growth and maturity vital to the whole church. Are you an active member of the body of Christ?

---

22 John MacArthur, The MacArthur New Testament Commentary on Ephesians (Moody Press, Chicago, 1986), p. 157.

I speak not of church attendance and church activities, but growing in relationship with Christ, and with each member of the body. I speak of becoming like Christ, performing in the world like Him, having His mind in a world that calls for us to conform to its thinking. Are you an active member of His body, actively influencing growth and maturity in the body of Christ? This is the win we seek. It is our pursuit. It will always be elusive in time, but guaranteed in eternity. *"Being confident of this very thing that He who has begun a good work in you will complete it until the day of Jesus Christ"* (Philippians 1:6). We win because Jesus won our victory through His incarnation, cross, resurrection, ascension, intercession, and return.

Although we have won, we are obliged to pursue the win. On Calvary, Jesus hit a grand slam, but we must run the bases. We run in hope. Hope is the certainty of the reality not yet experienced. For He who promised and provided the victory will bring it to fruition. We run from victory to victory, that is, we run within Jesus' victory towards the certainty of our victory—glorification. There is nothing or no one who can thwart what God has planned and purposed for those in Christ (see Romans 8:28-30). The beloved are those who are in right relationship with Jesus; those who have received Him become His children, destined for glory (see John 1:12, 13). There is nothing that will interfere with our realizing our destiny. We shall be with Jesus and like Him (see 1 John 3:1-3). This process of salvation begins in regeneration, grows through sanctification, and ends in glorification. It is the work of God from beginning to its conclusion. Salvation is for God to get the glory, and that Christ might be preeminent, the firstborn among us. We struggle at times to affirm His preeminence, but the day is coming when we will authentically be like Him. The question in the back of our minds is, if the win is guaranteed, why must we pursue it? Why pursue what is already won? The pursuit is driven by our love for God. We surrendered to the process of sanctification, moving us from glory to glory (see 2 Corinthians 3:18), not in fear but driven by His love. It is less of a pursuit towards salvation than it is a pursuit in salvation. We participate with the Holy Spirit in bring salvation to its ultimate end (see Philippians 2:12, 13). The Christian pursuit is not merely to know about Christ, but rather to become like Him. Christ apprehended Paul for the sole purpose of Paul's becoming like Him (see Philippians 3:7-14). Those who minister the Word of God must communicate this purpose to the hearers and doers of the Word. Transforming lives is the purpose of preaching and teaching. Reformation is not the goal. Transformation is our goal: being transformed into the image of Christ (see Romans 8:29). Therefore, *"We win when each member grows in relationship with Jesus, being, doing, thinking like Him, influencing growth and maturity in the body of Christ."*

ABOUT THE AUTHOR

Pastor Fred Campbell

Pastor Fred Campbell has served as Mt. Zion Baptist Church's pastor for over forty years, being one of the longest tenured pastors in the San Francisco Bay Area. His innovative and proven leadership has left an indelible mark, leading people towards spiritual maturity. Over the span of his Gospel ministry he's been a champion for discipleship, faith at home, education, empowering men, and more. Members enjoy his biblically sound preaching and teaching, humor, and personable demeanor. He is currently leading Mt. Zion in pursuing the win, where each member grows in relationship with Jesus and into maturity in the body of Christ.

Pastor Campbell is one of our nation's trailblazing leaders, serving in various capacities throughout his ministry. He's served in the California State Baptist Convention, Inc. in various leadership positions including Financial Secretary, Director of Christian Education, and Congress of Christian Education President. In 2002, under the mantra of "Building Healthy Churches," he became president of the California State Baptist Convention, guiding it in becoming a viable resource to local churches. Borne out his service to our state convention, Pastor Campbell is also a leader in the National Baptist Convention, USA, Inc. He served under the Shaw administration as historian, at-large board member under the Scruggs administration, and Chairman of the Board under the Young Administration.

Pastor Campbell has a deep passion for pastors, ministers, and their wives and provides wise counsel and support to pastors throughout the nation. In 2001, he and his wife Joyce founded Shepherd's Tent Ministries, a ministry that supports pastors, ministers, and their wives. This ministry now hosts the Word Conference, one of the premier conferences on the West Coast promoting biblical education and literacy.

He is a graduate of California Baptist University in Riverside, California, and Golden Gate Baptist Theological Seminary in Mill Valley, California.

Pastor Campbell was married to Joyce Elane Campbell for over forty-nine years before her passing in 2011. He has six children and five grandchildren.

CPSIA information can be obtained
at www.ICGtesting.com
Printed in the USA
LVOW03s0123260517
535906LV00004B/4/P

9 781939 225351